From Tragedy
to Blessing

*The Unforeseeable Journey of a
North Korean Refugee*

CHINKOOK LEE

Cover photo:
https://pixabay.com/en/sunset-yalu-river-north-korea-2339640/

ISBN: 198355524X
ISBN: 9781983555244

To my dear wife Teresa

And to my lovely grandchildren.

4/17/18
Dear Dr. Blakenlee
Thank you so much helping
me to get through with
my degree at WSU,

Chris

Author's Note

This is the story of my life.

I started writing a rough draft of this memoir after retiring in 2004 and often wondered whether I should finish it or not. But then I remembered a Korean proverb that says, "Tigers leave their hides when they die and human beings leave their writings." So I was inspired to continue writing this, as my main driving thought became, "What should I leave our five grandchildren so that they know more about and learn from their grandpa, especially as they get older and become adults?"

After many years of hesitation, I have finally decided to finish my story and share it.

I have had an unusual and unique past. Why do I say this? I think it will become clear to my grandchildren as they read about my life.

There are three themes in this memoir: first, as Koreans say, "Hardship during your youth cannot be bought with gold." I certainly had a very rough youth, but however hard it was, it was worth the experiences. Second, when you fail in your life, you need to try and try again to succeed. Never give up hope and work hard even after you fail. Third, when I had no hope in Korea, I left home for life in exile in America, and now towards the end of my life, I can say it was a hard journey but it ended with joy. We all know that there is no place like home, but as a second best option, there is no exile life better than living in America.

So my main hope is that our five grandchildren read this memoir when they are old enough and learn something from the lessons of my life. But along with my grandchildren's responses, I would welcome any feedback from anyone who reads this and wishes to give me their thoughts.

Chinkook Lee
chinkooklee@gmail.com
Aliso Viejo, CA

December 4, 2017
(67 years after my departure from home in Pyongyang)

CONTENTS

FOREWORD

We have always known that our dad was a North Korean refugee, and that his life featured a sad story about leaving Pyongyang when he was a young teenager, saying goodbye to his mother and then never seeing her again. On one hand, this was a very common story for my parents' generation of Koreans; all the first-generation Koreans we know have some sort of tragedy connected to their family life as a result of the Korean War. And yet, each and every story from the millions of people affected by the conflict is unique. After our dad retired, we encouraged him to take the time to tell his story more fully, for his own benefit but also so that we and others could learn more about what he experienced which has been so different from our own life experiences as second-generation Korean Americans.

Immortalizing stories into the written word illuminates details and gives them permanence and endurance. We now understand so much more than we ever did about our dad's early years, about what he suffered during wartime, and about his personal and professional challenges and accomplishments. This is no small gift; we wish all of our Korean-American friends could say that they had a similar cultural artifact in their own family that will last forever. Our dad has labored on this gargantuan effort, in his second language no less, off and on for more than ten years, and we are so grateful that he has taken the time to do so.

We also hope that others who do not know our dad personally will find his memoir illuminating, as it offers a window into the Korean-American experience that is both common to others' experiences while being unique at the same time. Since many stories have been disappearing as the first generation of Koreans passes into eternity, we are profoundly appreciative that our dad's and thus our family's story will endure for others to learn from, for as long as books exist.

Helen Lee and Brian K. Lee
Aliso Viejo, CA
December 2017

PROLOGUE

Joy.

At eighty years old, I'm full of joy. Somehow, I am. It's a miracle, really.

Joy is all around me. On this Thanksgiving Day, I am visiting my daughter Helen in Chicago to celebrate the holiday, and the sound of all my grandchildren is filling the house with noise, commotion, and laughter. And it all brings me joy. My whole family brings me joy, in spite of all of our ups and downs together, of which there are many as there are in any family.

Most importantly and most incredibly, my loving wife and all that she has done for me in our nearly fifty years of marriage brings me joy and is something I have appreciated more and more over the years. I thank God for bringing her to me. She has been the most incredible miracle throughout my eighty years of life so far.

I have to admit that my finding true joy is as much a surprise to me now as it would have been more than sixty years ago when I was going through a time in my life in which there was no more hope for joy.

But as I've learned repeatedly throughout my life, God works in mysterious ways. I now realize that every day since December 4, 1950, God has led me step by step closer to the joy I feel now. That was a key day in my life. It's one that still makes me sad and that reminds me of so much pain in my life. But over the years I've learned to commemorate it. And even if I can't 100 percent celebrate that day, I can appreciate it for where it ultimately led me.

This is the story of my life, highlighting key events and memories that I'd like to share with my grandchildren and my children. I feel it is important for them (and future generations in our family) to know about and learn from my past, so that they can apply key lessons learned in their own lives.

On December 4th, 1950, my father, brother, and I left my mother at home in

9

Pyongyang and started what became our refugee journey. I was thirteen years old, and I never saw my mother alive again after that day.

To those of you who know me well, yet perhaps did not know this fact about me, this probably explains a lot to you about why I am who I am. Leaving home at that age and then living as a war-torn refugee for the rest of my life without my mother's love had an immensely negative impact on my life. This created a recurring sadness in my life everyday thereafter.

For me, the single largest event that had an impact on my life was the Korean War. To this day, I wish that my entire family could have together fled Pyongyang together. It certainly could have been a much happier story for my entire family if we were all able to live in the newly-created South Korea. Perhaps we should have tried to relocate before the Korean War began in 1950. Certainly in hindsight we should have left together as a family for South Korea since that would have kept us together!

The war brought hardship and irreparable separation to my family. I had left home thinking that my father, brother, and I were going to find a new, safe home and would eventually return to home in Pyongyang within a couple of weeks. But that never happened. Instead, we became an all-too common tragedy that results from war.

But that's not the end of my story.

In 1989, thirty-nine years after I had left my home in Pyongyang, I was given the opportunity to not only come back to Pyongyang, but also to see my mother, **who I discovered was alive**! For years prior to that, I had searched for her and inquired about her only to be told time and time again that no one knew her whereabouts. Or that she had most likely passed away, or that she was indeed dead.

But on that trip to Pyongyang in 1989, I did not end up seeing my mother. Instead, I visited her grave in a remote rural mountain outside the city. Three months prior to my arrival, upon hearing the news that her second and youngest son was not only alive but actively looking for her, my mother passed away from a heart attack.

What a tragedy! It is almost unbelievable that this actually happened. I left her. I lost her, presumably for dead. I found her, she was alive. I went back to her at last. But when I finally arrived, she was dead. It sounds too unbelievable to be true, but it was.

This is a large part of my story--but not all of it. For all the tragedies that I have experienced, I have also experienced so many positive blessings.

That is also what I want to tell you about in this recounting of my life so far. As easy as it is to focus on the negatives and the hardships I faced (similar to so many war-torn refugees), I have also received many gifts, privileges, and miracles that I can call either destiny or, more likely, "God's will". There is a mystery to the journey of my life that I can only attribute to God's hand on my life. And ultimately, it is God who I must thank for the joy that I feel as I look back on my life.

Now let's start where it all began.

CHAPTER 1
MY EARLY YEARS (1937-1950)

Life in a Unified, But Japanese-Occupied Korea

I came into this world on December 20, 1937, born in a northern city called Pyongyang. Today, we know Pyongyang as the capital of North Korea, but that that time it was the second-largest city in a unified Korea that was under Japanese occupation. It was only in 1945 when the Japanese surrendered at the end of World War II that Korea was arbitrarily divided into two zones, the North and the South, by the United States and the Soviet Union because they could not agree on the creation of an independent, unified Korea. I lived in this newly-created North Korea for only five years, and yet I am considered a North Korean.

Japan ruled Korea for thirty-six years, from 1910-1945. When I was born, I learned and spoke only Japanese. My name was written in Japanese, not in Korean. My Japanese name was Hiromoto Jinkoku (Chinkook). Hiro came from the origin of our "Lee" family (permanent domicile) which is Kwangju, Kyunggi Do (Kyung Ki Province). "Kwang" is "Hiro" in Japanese. Moto comes from Japanese language. Since most Japanese names are in four Chinese characters, the Japanese took our family name Lee away and replaced it with Hiro and Moto to make my name four Chinese characters (廣本鎭國). My brother's name, therefore, is Hiromoto Jangkoku (Chungkook: 廣本貞國). I don't really remember if I spoke much Japanese since I was so young at the time, but I assume that I did since my brother could still speak Japanese well throughout his life. My brother said we also spoke Korean at home but it was not permitted officially!

At the end of World War II, Korea was liberated from Japan on August 15, 1945, and this turned my life back to being a Korean. Generally speaking, I had a very good, normal childhood life. I don't remember any particular ups or downs in my early stage of life, in my normal Korean family of four: my dad, mom, brother, and me.

Life in Communist North Korea

Unfortunately, the end of World War II also brought the intrusion of the big global nations (the U.S. and Russia) who were the ones that decided to split Korea: the North was occupied by Russia and the South by the U.S.

As things settled in Pyongyang after World War II, I started learning how to speak and write in Korean, but I was also forced to learn Russian right away. Since the Korean language is based on Chinese characters, I actually started learning three languages at once in these early years of my life: Korean, Russian, and Chinese.

My father was a supervisor of an electric power company in Pyongyang while my mother was a housewife. Like many Korean men, my dad seldom came home after work during the early evening for dinner. Usually he ate dinner out and came home after a few drinks. However, sometimes, he brought some good food for us, like doughnuts, candy, or cake, which he would wake us up to eat when he came home. I don't remember if we did any particular activities together as a family. I do remember that we often went out for naengmyun (cold Korean noodle soup), one of my favorite foods. But we never once had a family vacation. My brother and I spent most of our time at home with our mom.

My mother was a very caring woman and also a devoted Christian and a deacon at the West Pyongyang Methodist Church, and she took me to the church quite often. I don't think my brother went to church as often as I did. I attended a youth group worship similar to what many churches offer in the U.S. and in Korea. I still remember the church minister, Reverend Park, well since I attended church with my mom quite often. (More on Rev. Park to come.)

Since Pyongyang became the capital city of the North, my life then switched to the Russian Communist system and rule. This was another tragedy for people like me who were born in a small, powerless, but militarily-strategic country. This split occupation by the two superpowers became a tragedy for all Koreans, but certainly more so for those who happened to live in the northern part of the peninsula.

I was told that Russia invaded North Korea in the last minutes of World War II, but I was also told that the U.S. agreed to let Russia participate in the war at a very late stage. Since Japan at that time was already under the control of the U.S., Korea was the most logical country that Russia could enter to help end the war. How unlucky this was for Korea!

When North Korea became a Communist country, led by Kim Il-Sung, the majority of Korean people did not like the Communist Party. They demonstrated this by joining the Democratic Party, like my father, who rejected the Communist Party. However, this changed in the years that followed as Communist party leaders coerced citizens to join them and threatened to take away their jobs and livelihood if they did not.

When my father decided to leave home during the Korean War, like many others, he still belonged to the Democratic party. And this was a key reason for his seeking to relocate our family to the South.

Elementary School Years

My elementary school was fairly typical and in our classroom of about fifty boys (in Korea, as in Japan, boys and girls were not in the same classroom after the third grade), we had a stove right in the center of our room. During the cold winter weather, we burned coal to warm up the room throughout the day, and we kept our "bento" boxes (this was the Japanese name for a lunch box) on the stove to keep them warm. Whoever arrived at the classroom early had to put his bento on the bottom of the pile. Naturally, if yours was on the bottom, your lunch would get burned, but you had no choice if you arrived first. My lunch was on the bottom a few times and each time, half my lunch was burned.

Outside, there was a typical field with no grass for physical education classes. I walked about three miles to school from home: over a hill, a small mountain, a corn field, and more. Since the country and school were under the Communist regime, we had to pledge to Communism every morning before class, just like students recite the Pledge of Allegiance in the U.S.

Throughout my elementary school years, I was at the top of the class based upon my grades. One summer, I spent a month at Mt. Jang Back, located northeast of Pyongyang. It was a reward for achieving good grades, but it was also a brainwashing session. The leaders of the group taught us Communism about an hour every day. Meanwhile, whenever my dad came home and spent time with us, he told us how bad the Communist is and why he is not a member of Communist party.

Middle School Years

In North Korea, elementary school went up to the fifth grade, then you go to middle school. As in the U.S., your school is based on where you live. My school district was the Second Middle School of Pyongyang. It was about five miles away from home, and I either took a streetcar or walked all the way from school to home over a famous mountain hill called "Moran-bong." During this time, we moved from rural Pyongyang to a house at the bottom of a hill near the Pyongyang Stadium. Our home was walking distance from the Daedong River. As in elementary school, I was also at the top of my class in my first year in middle school. But I would end up finishing only that one year in North Korea.

I used to go up to the top of Moran-bong during the snowy winter with my handmade sled and ride all the way down to my home. But the war interrupted my golden age in terms of learning how to swim, skate, or participate in various other activities and sports.

I remember during Christmas vacations, since we now lived under a Communist regime that did not believe in any religion, we were required to attend school as usual. One year, we spent Christmas Eve at school, and when we were dismissed, the teacher told us not to go to church. However, my mother took me to church anyway, where I was caught by my school teacher who went there on purpose to catch any of his students that were attending. I don't know why he was assigned to our church, but this was an unfortunate incident for me. When we went back to school after winter vacation, I was called up in front of all the students in the gym, and I had to apologize for going to church. This was a typical Communist approach to encourage "self-criticism" when someone does something wrong. There were a few other students who were caught as well from other churches. I received a one-week suspension from school for that offense.

Communist propaganda and brainwashing were so prevalent that I know for certain that had I stayed in Pyongyang, I definitely would have been forced to become a strong Communist. Since I was at the top of the class, I received attention from school administrators and quite often I was selected to go to special meetings where most of the top students from different schools were gathered and which were used as brainwashing sessions for Communists. But I also didn't know much about the U.S., democracy, or capitalism since there was very little information about these ideologies in Pyongyang.

I spent five years in Communist, Russian-controlled North Korea. It was a tragedy for the unified Korean people to be arbitrarily split into two separate, and vastly different, countries, just as it was a tragedy before that to have the Japanese occupying our land and controlling us.

Reflecting back on this time of my life, with the Korean War approaching, I now see what a blessing it was that my Dad was fervently anti-Communist and that my Mom was a devoted Christian. This is what led us to leave our home in Pyongyang for a better future in South Korea. If only our entire family could have left together.

1949: The earliest picture I have of myself, from when I was twelve years old. This is the only picture that I brought from Pyongyang.

CHAPTER 2
STORIES OF WAR (1950)

The Korean War broke out on June 25, 1950 as Communist North Korea invaded the South. I think Kim Il-Sung's regime prepared well in advance to invade. I was at my grandmother's rural house with my brother since it was summer vacation. Pyongyang radio broadcasted that the forces of the South had crossed the 38th parallel line and invaded North Korea, so the North Korean army had no choice but to counterattack. But this was not true, and it is well documented that North Korea actually invaded South Korea. North Korea pushed the U.S. and South Korean armies all the way to the Nakdong River, bordering the Kyung Sang Buk Do in South Korea (a northern province of Kyungsang). The Nakdong River was a "do-or-die" border to the joint U.S. and South Korean army against the North Korean Army.

The commander of the U.S. army was General Douglas MacArthur, a rare five-star general. He came to Korea as the commander of the U.S. Pacific Army stationed in the Philippines. The South Korean army was very weak and not trained well to fight a war. Therefore, the U.S. army under General MacArthur was in charge of the war against the North Korean army. After about five months of fighting between the North Korean and U.S. armies at the Nakdong River, General MacArthur made a strategic decision to land military forces on the shore of Inchon, about 25 miles west of Seoul and about 200 miles north of Pyongyang.

After that, U.S. B-29 airplanes came to Pyongyang and dumped tons of propaganda papers announcing that U.S. forces had landed in Inchon. General MacArthur's strategy worked very well because while most of the North Korean army was further south, trying to cross the Nakdong River, the U.S.'s landing on Inchon cut the mainland of South Korea in half. There was no military defense in the middle of country. The North Korean army had not anticipated such a move and was not prepared to defend. They decided to retreat. This retreat continued all the way to the Chinese border.

When U.S. forces pushed the North Korean army to the northern border of Russia and China in December 1950, Communist China decided to help North Korea. The Chinese Red Army crossed the Dooman River, which runs along the border of China and North Korea. The U.S. forces under General MacArthur had a strategic decision to make: should they fight against the insurgent Chinese? Or should they retreat to South?

In the U.S., there was a big debate among politicians. President Truman and the Congress pondered what to do with the Red Army. General MacArthur wanted to bomb Manchuria, the Northeastern part of mainland China where many ethnic Koreans lived and where the Red Army was crossing the Dooman River. President Truman feared expanding the war which wasn't politically popular in the U.S. He was also concerned about another possible World War. In the end, Truman decided not to escalate the war and ordered U.S. forces to retreat to South.

General MacArthur insisted that bombing Manchuria was the right course of action and refused to obey President Truman's order of retreat. President Truman then was forced to fire General MacArthur who retired from the army and returned home. At the joint session of the U.S. Congress, he gave his famous final speech saying, "Old soldiers will never die but will just fade away."

Historians debate who was right or wrong during the Korean War and what would have happened had the U.S. bombed northern China then. Did Truman make the right decision? Had the U.S. taken the more aggressive step, that could have escalated the war; the U.S.—with a much more superior military at that time—could have defeated the Chinese easily. If so, Taiwan, where many refugees from mainland Communist China lived and are still living, could have taken part in the war and invaded mainland China. Had this happened, I believe China now would be a free country. President Truman's decision not to bomb Manchuria was probably a key event that led to the divided Korea that we see now.

In 2010, 60 years after the start of the Korean War, I went go back to Korea and one of my old high school friends took me to the Korean War zone at the Nakdong River. He explained to me how the U.S. and South Korean army were able to defeat the North Korean there. As I visited the war memorials there, I had a wave of very mixed emotions. On the one hand I was so grateful that the the North Korean Army had been defeated. They were the aggressor, they were oppressive, they were deserving of the defeat. But on the other hand, even though I only lived in Communist North Korea for five years, Pyongyang was my home, it was where I grew up, and this war had caused so much pain, suffering, and destruction to the people there, including my own family.

The Seventeen-Day Journey That Changed My Life

On December 4, 1950, as U.S. forces started to retreat to the South, my dad, brother and I packed our belongings, left home, and started our journey to Seoul as refugees. I was nearly thirteen years old, and my brother was fifteen years old. Since I was very young, this decision to leave home and escape to the South was my dad's. Many Korean families and men who lived in the North did the same during the early days of the war. The Communist North Korean government treated its people very poorly, and many citizens hated this government even though they could not say it openly.

We started walking to Seoul, the capital of South Korea, about 130 miles south of Pyongyang. Most refugees walked in that direction without any particular destination planned ahead of time. However, we had an uncle who had left Pyongyang a long time ago and settled in Seoul. My dad had his whereabouts and our aim was to find him.

We left our mother at home because we thought that we would return within a week or two after we found our uncle and a new place in the South to call home.

I have regretted this decision ever since. And this one decision would change our lives, my life, forever. What were we thinking? Why were we so confident that we would return in a couple weeks' time? Why were we willing to risk leaving my mother and other family behind and separate our family during a war?

This shows how limited people's thinking can be, and how just one decision made with such incomplete knowledge can result in a lifetime of regret.

I also think that there is another reason my mother decided to stay in Pyongyang. She did not want to leave her two brothers behind. Her younger brother had been drafted into the North Korean Army and was deployed to the north, and her other older brother was a Communist who went north after the U.S. army landed in Inchon. I think that my mom's decision to stay at home was strongly influenced by her desire to see her brothers again.

We never thought that "couple of weeks' separation" would become a permanent one! However, in hindsight, my mom's desire to see her two brothers was part of the mistakes we made that resulted in our permanent separation. Of course, I can't blame my mom for her decision to remain in Pyongyang, because my mom never believed our separation would be permanent.

So we said goodbye to our mom, saying, "Mom, we'll see you in a couple weeks" and started our seventeen-day walk on foot to Seoul. As I mentioned earlier, we were not the only family to choose to do so, since many families only sent part of their family initially and typically it was only the men who left. Some lucky families left Pyongyang all together as a group. But millions of North Koreans left their wives and women in the North, thinking as we did that they would be able to return later and then bring the rest of our families to our new homes in the South.

But this seemingly temporary "goodbye" was the last time I would see my mother.

Crossing the Daedong River

On our first day after departing Pyongyang, we walked about ten miles and then struggled to cross the Daedong River the rest of the day because the bridge had been bombed and was destroyed. People moved up and down the north shore of the river all day looking for a spot where they could cross. We wandered up and down the shoreline for about ten hours on the northside of the river until finally someone jumped into the water. It was December and the river was almost frozen. Pieces of ice were flowing downstream, but we felt we didn't have any choice but to follow the leader who had started crossing. So we jumped into the water and started to wade through with all our heavy belongings on our back. The water was about waist deep but flowing slowly enough so that we could keep our belongings over the water and mostly dry and still cross safely. It was a cold, dark evening and chunks of ice hit our bodies while we crossed.

I still remember that it took about forty minutes to cross to the south shore of the river. We were freezing cold, wet, and bloody from being hit by ice when we crossed. My body was cut and bruised, but there was no severe damage, and I just wiped the blood away as best as I could. Since it was dark, we just undressed on the spot and changed into dry clothing as quickly as possible.

One of the rewards for making it across the cold river was that the U.S. army greeted us on the other side of the shore of the Daedong River. They gave us some rations to eat and we received cans of tuna fish. The problem was we didn't know how to open them. Later we found out that the openers were on the bottom of the cans. But we didn't know this at the time, as we had never seen canned food like this! We were very hungry having had nothing to eat all day, so we found rocks on the shore and tried our best to use them to open the tuna fish cans. We worked to make a hole in the can and once we did that we just used our fingers to get the tuna out from the can. It was only when we finished eating, that we even noticed that our fingers were bleeding because they were scratching the sharp edges of the metal can.

We wrapped up our bloody fingers with clothes and we unloaded our blankets from our backpacks to create makeshift beds on the gravel shore on the south side of the river. From here, we could still see the lights of Pyongyang in the distance on the other side of the river. Due to our exhaustion, somehow we were able to sleep in the freezing cold weather on that first night of our journey to Seoul, just a few miles away from our home and away from my mom.

The next morning the rest of our journey to Seoul began. Sometimes we slept on the street and other times in empty houses. Thankfully, weather was not a factor; there was no rain or snow that I can recall on our trek to Seoul, and the temperatures became warmer as we traveled south.

We did however encounter an attack by the U.S. Air Force on our convoy. I witnessed people and animals (cart-pulling oxen) killed by machine-gun fire from the fighter jets flying over us. Those of us who survived were very lucky. We would run for the nearest ditch, lie down and just wait for the firing to end. It was confusing to see the U.S. aircraft firing at us, we were clearly civilians! And just days earlier weren't those same army soldiers giving us food and rations??

After our seventeen-day journey, we arrived at the northern tip of Seoul on December 20, 1950. It was snowing and it was also my thirteenth birthday. We had walked on foot for all those days only to arrive in Seoul where nobody was waiting for us. But we couldn't stay there long because the Chinese and North Korean Army were closing in on Seoul and so we had to retreat further south. So we packed again, jumped on top of a crowded freight train roof and went further south to the city of Taegu. I had no idea that I would end up spending more of my life than I was expecting in that city.

CHAPTER 3
REFUGEE LIFE BEGINS (1951-1957)

It was now 1951, and our refugee life had begun in Taegu. We somehow found my dad's stepsister (고모) in Taegu by accident, and my dad was excited to have her to stay with us. I think we met her at the Yankee (Korean slang for "Americans") market where we opened a small store to try and start making a living. Since we didn't know anyone in Taegu, we were living at the time at the Taegu train station waiting room with about 30 other people.

The "Yankee Market"

Without my mother, but now with my aunt with us, the four of us started our new lives in Taegu as refugees. We stayed in the Taegu train station waiting room for about two weeks. We slept on the floor since the benches along the wall were all occupied by those who arrived before us. During the daytime we all went to work selling goods in the "Yankee market." I sold American cigarettes while my brother and my dad sold other goods that we purchased from GIs. We then moved into a duplex which was located quite far away from the Yankee market, across a rice paddy field. Our main food, once a day in the evening, was squid soup. Winter was squid-catching season in the Sea of Japan, so squid was plentiful and cheap. Every night my aunt would make soup for us, which we would eat with rice.

After living for about two months in the duplex, my father found a friend who he knew from Pyongyang. He and his family had moved to Seoul right after Korea's liberation from Japan, sometime after the year 1945 and were well-settled in Seoul. They owned a hosiery factory with equipment they had brought from North Korea.

He and my dad had been friends when they were children in Pyongyang; I called him "Uncle." Uncle invited us to come and live in his house, which was already crowded with his family and his

23

brother's family. The only place we could move into was in was their attic. We did so and lived there quite a while.

Uncle helped us out quite a bit. He even made us a grill using one of the big metal oil tanks they used in their factories. This was a good grill to bake sweet potatoes. We put that grill onto a pull cart and took it to a street corner about thirty minutes away from Uncle's home. My dad and I baked sweet potatoes and sold them; it was such a cold winter that they sold well. Every morning and evening we would make the half-hour trek, pushing and pulling the heavy cart.

While my dad and I were selling baked sweet potatoes on the street, my brother continued to go to the Yankee market to sell goods. The Yankee market grew out of an empty lot that refugees flooded to start their small shops. They would put up tents and a table and claim spots for themselves, and my brother was able to eventually find a spot at that market.

1951: "Hot summer at Yankee Market" is what I wrote in blue - I'm sitting at the far right.
(r) 2010: Yankee Market - where my dad's old store used to be.

In 2010, I visited Taegu and one of my old high school friends took us to see the Yankee market. We even saw where my dad and brother had their small tables to sell their goods. Sixty years later the market is still there! But naturally it is very different now with fancy shops around.

By the time the summer of 1951 arrived, we had made enough money to move out from Uncle's attic and rent a two-bedroom house. Our aunt lived with us there until later when she married the younger brother of one of dad's friend from Pyongyang.

During this period, Uncle asked me about my dad's birthday. I didn't know it then, but my brother knew it was August 3. After finding this out from my brother, Uncle gave my dad a big birthday party on his 42nd birthday in 1951. After a few drinks, my dad started to cry and cry, thinking about my mom and our sad Korean War tragedy. From that day forward, I never forgot my dad's birthday and always sent him some kind of gift until he passed away. It was sad that my dad lived without my mom and also had to take over much of both parents' job now that we were in Taegu and trying to move forward with our lives. He was a good dad. Unfortunately however, human beings are not perfect, and my dad would make mistakes later that would affect us significantly.

We were relatively successful at the Yankee market, which became a well-established market due to the influx of refugees, and the various goods we mostly purchased from GI's sold very well. Dad was then able to start a men's clothing shop there, and he made enough money so that we were able to rent a larger two-bedroom house. As we settled into life in Taegu. I don't recall spending much time thinking about my former life in the north. Mainly, we were trying just to survive these difficult conditions together.

Continuing With Middle School and then High School

With my father now generating a reasonable income, he was able to send my brother and me to Choong Ang Middle School in September 1951. This school was opened for North Korean refugees who were a year or two behind due to the war. The school didn't ask for any papers or proof of eligibility. Naturally, most students who entered this school were not well prepared. They, like me, were refugees and hadn't grown up normally. Most of them were working on the street, as I had during my first year of what was supposed to be middle school.

I finished middle school in two years and went to Keisung High School in 1953, after taking the entrance exam and passing. I was lucky to be admitted to this prestigious missionary high school. I was the only one from Choong Ang who was accepted to Keisung High School, which had very few students from North Korea;

most students were locals. Therefore, my North Korean accent wasn't appealing to the local southerners and I didn't make many friends during the three years I spent at Keisung. Most friends that I made were from a church I attended later on, when I was one of the high school chorus members, many of whom were also from Keisung.

I also had a rough start academically, particularly in English. This was because I never studied English when I was in school at Pyongyang; I'd only studied Russian. Also Choong Ang, the middle school I attended, really wasn't an academically rigorous school. Its goal was to help those unfortunate young people who missed school for a time because they had to work for a living. As a result, I wasn't well-prepared to meet the challenge of a good high school such as Keisung.

When I entered Keisung, I was three years behind the other students in English. I could catch up on other subjects, but it wasn't easy to catch up in English. I still remember a time when the English teacher asked me to read a few paragraphs of a story, I pronounced "only" as "one-ly" and the teacher announced loudly, "I have never heard a student pronouncing 'only' as 'one-ly.'" He was really upset. Without even knowing the English alphabet, I had to start reading, writing, and speaking in English class five days a week. However, I studied hard and eventually was able to overcome all those obstacles, graduating in the top ten percent of my class (23rd out of 250 students).

Even so, being in that top ten percent was no guarantee that I would have an easy or good life. In fact, I was about to endure yet another big disappointment that I thought would change my life for the worse forever.

1953: Sixteen years old.
(r) 2010: Keisung High School classmates (Jung Chang Lee and Chul Soo Kang) during my visit to Taegu.

My Christian Life

While I had some exposure to Christianity in Pyongyang when I attended the children's service at West Pyongyang Methodist Church, my real Christian life started in Taegu when I entered Keisung High School. The school had Bible class once a week, a revival worship week at least twice a year (during which no classes were in session), and also all of the students attended local churches. I attended Choong Ang Presbyterian Church because it was close to where we lived. I joined the high school Bible class and also the high school chorus as a bass singer. We usually sang at the Sunday evening worship or on Wednesday nights.

Going to church again reminded me of my mother, so I was always wondering how and what she was doing. Perhaps she was praying to the same God I was praying to, hoping we would be reunited someday.

During this time, there was a deacon whose name was Mr. Park who was in charge of the high school group. He was a very sincere Christian who wanted for us to do good for society as part of our Christian lives. He had us go to Taegu Train Station and crusade in front of the refugees and homeless people who slept there. So we sang together there, distributed Bibles and provided people with food. Since I remembered my own two-week stay at the train station when we arrived in Taegu a few years before, I really enjoyed this crusade and worked very hard on it.

Deacon Park saw me working sincerely to help spread the love of Jesus Christ to these people. Later, Mr. Park asked me to work for him part-time delivering Christian newspapers on the weekends. I was able to meet many pastors around the city of Taegu as I visited their homes or churches to deliver the papers. I still remember a number of them very well and was lucky to meet some of them later in my life in Seoul and in the U.S.

I also became acquainted with a high school senior, Mr. Chang Kun Chung, who was the president of the high school student group. He was a sincere Christian with whom I spent many hours and days with, along with Mr. Park, as we discussed how we should devote our lives to Christianity. Once a month, our group had a special worship on Sunday evening and many times Mr. Chung asked me to lead prayer. My faith grew as I spent many hours with both Mr. Park and Mr. Chung.

1956: Choong Ang Presbyterian Church with Reverend Kim.
2010: A new church on that same site.

My Father's Life and Our Relationship

While we were in Taegu, my dad decided to remarry and I did not get along well with my stepmom. She also had two other children. One example of our problems was that my new stepmother did not like that I would not call her "mother". This was very hard for me. I felt that calling a stepmother the name "mother" should come

28

out naturally from my heart, not be forced. My brother on the other hand was always a man of reconciliation and he adjusted well to our new stepmother. But I just couldn't!

When my brother graduated from high school and left Taegu for Seoul to go to college, my dad realized that I couldn't get along well with his new wife so that he decided to let me have a separate living arrangement. He rented me a room nearby the church I attended. It was also nearby where my dad lived with his new wife and the two other kids. I don't recall how long I lived there alone, but I remember that I would eat at their house and go back to my place to sleep alone.

1950's: Earliest picture of my dad who was born on August 3, 1919.

1987: At the 38th parallel with my dad.

1991: Bowing to my dad at His grave with my half-brother, Kyungkook Lee, and his wife.

The front of my dad's grave which says, "Looking to the North where my home is."

The back of my dad's grave. From right to left are the names of my older brother, his wife and underneath are his children's names; the third from the right are me, my wife, and our children.

My Dad's Second Marriage in South Korea

I finished high school and moved to Seoul which resulted in less contact with my new stepmother. But I also didn't have any communication with my dad for quite a long time. During this period, my brother was in military service and I lived in Seoul in a house as a student teacher (가정교사). In Korea, many wealthy families have a student teacher in their home to supplement their children's education. One day, I met my brother at the Seoul train station when he was on his way to the war zone at the 38th parallel, and he told me where my dad was.

My dad had left his new wife and was now living in Pusan. One of his friends, who was also from North Korea, had a t-shirt factory. He was helping my dad start a new business selling t-shirts. My dad's friend also introduced my dad to a new woman who was much younger than him.

He married her, and she became his second wife in South Korea. She just recently passed away and was a very nice woman. My dad died at the age of 87, but without her caring for him, I think he would have passed away much earlier. My brother and I have talked about this fortunate event in my dad's life many times. My brother and I have always been so thankful to her for taking such good care of our father. After they were married, they had two sons, Kyung Kook and Kwang Kook—my half-brothers. Until her death, she lived in Seoul, and Kyung Kook especially took good care of her.

While I didn't have too much interaction with my second stepmother since I was in the U.S., my dad showed very happy with this marriage. I discerned this whenever I visited home in Seoul and also from talking with my brother. As time flew by and my two half brothers became adults, Kyung Kook (the older brother) became a very successful CEO in the television industry, as an inventor of TV technology. And, he and his wife lived with my parents and took care of them.

He used his experiences as an engineer at the KBS (Korean Broadcasting Service) after getting an electrical engineering degree from Seoul National University. When he had an idea of how to make a TV screen brighter and clearer, he resigned from KBS and set up his own company, TVLogic. His company grew tremendously over time and eventually went public company. When the IPO (Initial Public Offering) came out, the company stock prices soared from the beginning, and after few years he sold TVLogic stock to a bigger company at a huge profit.

1980s: My dad, my two half-brothers, my stepmother (see yellow arrow) and her mother.

CHAPTER 4
HARDSHIPS IN SEOUL (1957-1963)

Hopeless for a Time

Human beings always live with great hopes. Hope for a better life, hope for a good family, hope for good children, hope for God's blessings, hope that everything will turn out the way we wanted. Living without hope is no different from being dead. Many young people from regional high schools came to Seoul every March with joy and hope because they were accepted to one of the prestigious universities in Seoul.

I came to Seoul without admission to one of those universities. But I could still have hope for my future since I finished Keisung High with a pretty good class standing. Keisung High was a very reputable school, and many graduates went to good colleges in Seoul. My class standing was high enough that my teacher recommended that I try the entrance exam at Seoul National University (SNU). But I did not pass, which at the time left me with a hopeless life in Seoul.

In Korea, your future and career can be very dependent upon which university you graduate from. Your future and career path can be somewhat predictable if you graduate from a university such as SNU. But if you fail to enter the first-ranked colleges, you can have a very difficult future and career path in front of you. This was true back then and I think it is even more true today.

My life could have been very different had I gotten accepted into a first-level university. I probably would have finished four years at one of these universities, then gotten a job and settled down in Seoul rather than coming to the U.S. My teacher's recommendation for me to apply to SNU was based on Keisung's records of acceptance in the past, and he thought that I had a chance to pass the exam.

In hindsight, I am very grateful that I did not pass. But at the time, I was devastated by this turn of events in my life.

My Soongsil College Life (1957-1961)

I had to adjust my plans last-minute since I had not gotten into SNU. My brother was already in Seoul, so I was able to stay with him and make new plans. I decided to apply to Soongsil College, because it would be easy for me to get in as I had a transcript and recommendation. Soongsil was located in a remote suburb of Sangdodong which is across the Han River from Seoul. However, because it was in a rural community, there was no good transportation to get there. Furthermore the Han River bridge was destroyed during the war, so getting to school could take more than an hour.

In economics, there was only one full time professor, and all others were lecturers from various universities in town, and mostly from SNU College of Commerce. One of the well-known SNU professors who lectured at Soongsil was Byun Hyung Yoon whom I would meet later at Vanderbilt University.

One extracurricular activity that I did participate in was an English class called the "Vine Club" which was organized by missionaries from the Christian Children's Fund headquartered in Richmond, Virginia. This club met every Thursday night at the missionary's resident on the foothill of Namsan and had about twelve to fifteen students, from Ewha Women's University, SNU, Soongsil and a few other universities. We read the Bible and then discussed the meaning of the specific verses we read. This conversational club helped me to learn how to listen in English and later would help me pass the English portion of the study abroad test conducted by the Ministry of Education.

1960: 22 years old.
Middle: Vine Club members
Right: Soongsil graduation with my classmates, Key T. Kim and Elder Taeyoon Park.

Life in the Korean Army (1961-1963)

After graduating from Soongsil, I joined the Korean army in 1961 for two reasons. First, there was no worthwhile job for me to pursue with only my bachelor's degree from Soongsil. Second, everybody had to fulfill military obligations before pursuing a career. This is still the case for Korean young men. We had to serve a minimum of three years in the military before moving on with our lives and careers.

During my one-year service in the Korean army, I was granted occasional vacation time. On one vacation, I decided to take a study-abroad examination conducted by the Ministry of Education of the Korean Government. I didn't have any specific plan to go to abroad, but I just felt that I had to do something different because I did not think I could get a suitable job when I got out of the army after doing my three years of service. Most graduates from Soongsil went to divinity school since Soongsil was a very conservative Christian school.

The required tests were in Korean history and English. Korean History was easy, but the English test was difficult for me. We had to pass Composition, Grammar, Conversation, and Writing. I do not know how I did it, but I passed both the Korean History and the English exam. Most candidates fail on Conversation; the examiner, who was an American woman, would read a one-page story twice and we had to answer questions based on what she read aloud. My guess is that my experiences at Soongsil, where I would attend weekly gatherings with American missionaries, reading and answering Bible study questions, helped prepare me for this part of the exam.

Several months after I went back to the army compound, I was called in by the lieutenant colonel to his office. He informed me that an order came from the army headquarters that I would be discharged the next month. He congratulated me but also informed me that this discharge was not an typical discharge after fulfilling my duty, but a special one-year "study abroad" discharge. This meant that I had to go study abroad within a year. Otherwise, I would have to return to the army for another two years of service.

After I was discharged from the army, I spent most of my time in the U.S. Embassy Information Service Bureau where I could find graduate school university catalogs and began filling out applications. A few months later, I received a letter from the registrar of one university which said, "Congratulations, Miss Lee, you are accepted to our graduate school program." Apparently, it was a women's university. I must have applied to a women's university by accident!

But the real miracle came from Vanderbilt University. Somehow they had accepted me into their master's program in economics. This was exactly what I needed to get my I-20 visa to go study abroad in the U.S. At the time, I knew very little about Vanderbilt. I am very grateful that they gave me a chance and played a huge role in getting me to the U.S. and positioning me for a good future.

Amongst my fellow South Korean army men.

Hope Returns as I Head to America (June 1963)

At first, the thought of leaving for America felt like yet another tragedy to me at the time. I would think to myself that if it had not been for the Korean War, I would not have to go to America. And my family would not be separated. Only later would I truly realize the blessing I had received. And as difficult as it was to leave Korea, to leave my homeland, to leave my family yet again, I did start to experience a sense of hope.

I had hope that I could restart my life in America. It was a very vague idea, because I didn't have a well-conceived plan to come to America. I just wanted to leave Seoul because in my mind there was no hope for me in Korea. I am very grateful that my dad worked hard with his T-shirt business and was able to save enough money to buy me a one-way ticket to Los Angeles ($307 back then).

I left Seoul in June 1963 with $100 in my pocket given to me by my dad who said, "You will have your own life in the U.S. Don't plan on coming back home to Korea. You have to be successful in America."

My last day at home before departing for America, where nobody would be there to welcome me, my dad came to my room to spend the night with me, my dad holding me in his arms as he cried. He was sending his son to an uncertain world, and we had a very emotional night. This was only the second time that I saw my dad cry. I first saw him crying when our uncle gave him a birthday party in Taegu.

I cried with him and told him not to worry about me. I reminded him that I had no future in Korea, and the only thing I could do was to go to America, which now represented a land of hope for me.

CHAPTER 5
MY LIFE IN EXILE (1963-1966)

Arriving and Surviving in the U.S.

A Korean proverb says, "If you get to the beginning you are halfway there."

I began my life in the U.S. with the $100 in my pocket that my dad had given to me and was supposed to go directly to Vanderbilt which was in Nashville, Tennessee. But instead I had routed my connecting flight from Seoul to San Francisco to then take me to Los Angeles. I had to earn enough money to go to graduate school, and I would go to Los Angeles to try and do this. Many young Koreans ended up skipping their study abroad programs and just staying in the U.S. illegally. But I was planning to try to make some money and then leave for Vanderbilt. Hopefully by merely arriving in Los Angeles, I would be halfway to my goal of making enough to get to graduate school.

When I left Korea, Dr. Shungnak L. Kim, the president of Soongsil University at that time, gave me a note to go to Reverend Noh's home in Los Angeles. (Unfortunately, I cannot remember Rev. Noh's first name.) Dr. Kim had previously lived in Los Angeles almost all his life, he had earned a Ph.D. in theology, and he had been a Presbyterian minister in Los Angeles. Thus, he was very well known in Los Angeles Korean community. After living in Los Angeles, he became the president of Soongsil when I was senior at the university. He was also born in Pyongyang and his dad (Rev. Sundoo Kim) had been a very well known Presbyterian minister there. Dr. Kim's note told me to go to Rev. Noh's house and asked for his help to get me settled in Los Angeles. So after arriving, I took a taxi from the airport and asked the driver to go to Rev. Noh's address. Taxi fare was $5, so I already spent $5 out of the $100 in my pocket.

When I arrived at Rev. Noh's house, he wasn't expecting me since he'd never met me and there was no advance warning of my arrival from Dr. Kim. I gave him Dr. Kim's note. When he read the note, Rev. Noh took me in and suggested that I get some rest, which I did.

Rev. Noh's help at the beginning of my American life made the early days of my transition significantly easier. He fed me and the next day he took me to a Japanese-American employment service where I was sent to the CBS record printing company. I was one of four people who took a brief test and I was the only one who was selected to start work the next week. I paid two-thirds of my first month's salary to the employment service. Rev. Noh then helped me find a place to live. He took me to a place where another Korean immigrant lived so that I could live with him and share the rent. Rev. Noh also found a carpool for me to take me to work starting on Monday. That's the way my life in Los Angeles began. How grateful I am to Rev. Noh (and Dr. Kim) for their help in starting a life in the U.S.!

It was summertime, but the CBS record-producing plant was already busy preparing for Christmas records. That's why I was able to get a job with them. But after a few months of working there, the busy season was over, and I was laid off. So I had to go to the Japanese employment agency again, and I was directed to go to a Japanese-American furniture store, Tamula & Co, which hired me as a delivery person. The driver spoke fluent Japanese and almost all of their customers were Japanese-American. Unfortunately, I hurt my back while I was working there. As soon as they noticed that I was hurt, they fired me.

So I had to go to the employment agency again. This time I got a job as a shipping and receiving clerk at a textile wholesale store. My job was to make cuts from rolls of textile based on received orders and to ship it out on trucks every evening. Luckily, that was my last job before leaving for Vanderbilt. I had made enough money and was ready to move on.

From Los Angeles to Nashville, Vanderbilt University (1964)

Nashville was my "promised land" because Vanderbilt accepted me into its master's degree program in economics. I was being given the chance to earn an advanced degree in America.

At the end of August 1964, I took a cross-country journey on a Greyhound bus from Los Angeles to Nashville, Tennessee. It took five days and nights, changing drivers five times on the same bus. This was another turning point of my life because had I stayed in Los Angeles, my status may have ended up as an illegal immigrant. If it had, I most likely would not have gotten a master's degree and also almost certainly would not have worked in the federal government later on.

When I arrived at Vanderbilt, most foreign students there were on government scholarships or government-sponsored Ford Foundation fellowships. Only a few were like me, coming with only a tuition waiver. I lived in Wesleyan Hall, a dorm for graduate students. I often cooked on a hot plate in my room (which was against the rules), heating Campbell soup and spaghetti noodles. I remember paying a dollar for five cans! I could eat on roughly $25 per month.

On Friday evenings the few Korean students who attended Vanderbilt gathered at the University Methodist Church and used their kitchen to cook Korean food. One of the Korean students in the divinity school was a Methodist minister from Korea and was also the caretaker of the church. We made simple Korean food; we bought cabbage, green onion, garlic, salt, pepper, and soy sauce. We soaked cabbage with salt water for a while and then mixed it with garlic and peppers. This made instant kimchi. We also sometimes made fish soup. We looked forward to that great supper every Friday evening.

I had a rough to start my master's program because Vanderbilt was a prestigious school and most students in my graduate program were studying for their Ph.D diplomas. They also came from very good colleges or universities with strong undergraduate backgrounds. Only a few of us were in the master's program. I also didn't have a strong economics background from college as back then I'd had no plans at the time to pursue a graduate degree in this field.

So that first year was really hard. When I sat in the classroom, I couldn't understand what the professors were saying, since my English was still very poor. I was not able to ask any questions since I did not know what professors were saying!

I remember that one professor who taught us Economic Growth had a soft voice as well as a foreign accent. I just couldn't understand him at all. One day in the class everybody was submitting something to the professor. I didn't know what was going on. Apparently he gave us a reading assignment when we'd met for class the last time. I missed the assignment since I couldn't understand him well. When everybody submitted a paper I approached the professor and told him that I misunderstood his assignment in our last class. He replied, "That's your problem." I ended up with a "C" grade from him.

In my master's program, there were three Korean students. Two were from the College of Commerce at Seoul National University, where I failed to gain entry years ago. Another was Professor Byun, a professor at the College of Commerce, SNU who, as I previously mentioned, had also moonlighted by teaching at Soongsil University. I'd taken two courses with him while I was at Soongsil.

He came to Vanderbilt to get his master's and his Ph.D. During the second semester he and I decided to move out from the graduate student dorm because it was so expensive and to share an apartment. I cooked and he washed the dishes. Since he had a fellowship, he was in a much better financial position than me. Professor Byun had parents who were from North Korea, as my dad was, and so we had a lot in common.

Two of my other Korean classmates at Vanderbilt were Kie Wook Lee and Suk Joon Suh. Both of them were very smart and promising stars in the Korean government when they returned after receiving their degrees. Mr. Lee finished his Ph.D. while Mr. Suh decided to return home after earning his master's degree. Mr. Lee and I became close friends. After finishing his degree he went to teach at the University of Southern Mississippi for a while and then went to Seoul to teach at one of the universities there. Later he became the Deputy Minister of Finance. Unfortunately in 1983, he and twenty-one other people died in Rangoon, the capital of Burma, as a result of a terrorist incident when three bombs went off trying to kill President Chun Doo Hwan. The other classmate, Suk Joon Suh, became a Vice Prime Minister and also died at the Rangoon incident.

A snowy day at Vanderbilt with some of my fellow foreign students.

Getting my Master's Degree at Vanderbilt University and Heading West (1964-1966)

At Vanderbilt, I barely earned my master's, but by God's grace I did! The program had been a full-year program which included a summer session. So I finished my degree within 18 months. After I finished, however, I didn't know what to do. I couldn't go back to Korea because it would be difficult to find a worthwhile job. During this period, Korea was still economically poor and there weren't many jobs for U.S.-educated people.

To stay in the U.S., I either had to maintain an F-1 (student visa) or go home. So even though I hadn't planned on pursuing a Ph.D., I felt forced to at least enroll in a part-time Ph.D. program while also working part-time to make a living.

I began a job search in the U.S., mostly focused on teaching positions, but I also had to find a school where I could continue studying for my Ph.D. to secure my visa from the school. I landed a job at St. Martin's College, a Catholic school near Olympia, Washington. Miraculously, despite my struggles at Vanderbilt, I was able to enroll at the University of Washington (UW), thanks to professor Dean Worcester, the graduate student advisor who accepted me into the Ph.D. program on a part-time basis. Since the teaching at St. Martin's was mostly done in the evenings, I would be able to simultaneously take the minimum credit hours required by immigration rules and begin school at UW in the fall.

So in March 1966, I arrived in Seattle and settled into an apartment near the University of Washington campus. I never thought that I would pursue a Ph.D., because I had assumed my educational background to be weak. However, circumstances forced me to enroll and so I began my pursuit of a Ph.D. This is another example of how life can take you down unexpected paths. I never imagined I would be headed on another journey to a completely different part of the country. And I would also be headed toward some big life changes that would have a huge impact on my future.

CHAPTER 6
SALES, THEN A NEW START
(1966-1968)

The Hardest Profession on Earth

Before I started at UW and at St. Martin's College, that summer I decided to join three other Korean students to sell dictionaries as College Student Salesman recruits. We were recruited by the Southwestern Publishing Company in Nashville. With a student visa, we were allowed to work full time during our summer vacation.

Mr. Im was the leader of our group, and this was his third summer going to Nashville to sell the Webster's College Edition Dictionary. The two other students who were at UW before me had heard many positive stories from Mr. Im and had decided to join him. So I joined them as well. This also gave me the opportunity to revisit Nashville.

After four days of training in Nashville, we headed to Amarillo, Texas. The most memorable information I still remember from the training was how to avoid dog-biting! The company gave us a free briefcase to carry a few dictionaries, and they taught us how to use it if a dog came after us when we knocked at a door.

Mr. Im instructed us to go to Amarillo's downtown office buildings and knock on the doors of CEOs and presidents of various banks. That first morning as a salesman, we had high hopes of selling many dictionaries. The price was $10 and our profit was 50 percent, so $5 per dictionary. And of course, we had to pay all our expenses out of our profits. We divided our territories at the hotel room, and after getting off the city bus we all headed in different directions. We wished each other good luck and promised to meet later for dinner at a local Chinese restaurant.

When we gathered at the Chinese restaurant, everyone was exhausted and had gloomy faces. Three of us didn't make any sales at all! We couldn't figure out how to get a meeting with any CEOs or presidents of banks. Mr. Im told us that this was natural. He said to try again the next day with positive thinking.

"Also," he said, "don't talk to the secretary. Just say 'Hi' and walk into the CEO's office." He explained, "A CEO will never turn you down once you are in his office. He will at least try to see who you are and why you are there. At that point you just go ahead and give the sales talk you learned at training. Just leave the dictionary on his desk and walk out. If you do, they will pay for it or they'll leave money with the secretary which you can collect next morning."

We tried another couple of days without any success. Therefore, on the third night at the Chinese restaurant, the three of us told Mr. Im that we were going to try a residential area. Mr. Im said sales would be much better in office buildings because many CEOs would buy our dictionary out of sympathy, knowing that we were trying to earn money for our college education. However, the three of us made the decision to try a residential area. Mr. Im advised us not to go to poor residential areas since they wouldn't have money to buy dictionaries.

So we tried a wealthy neighborhood where we thought many CEOs' houses were located. The problem was that nobody came to the door. Or if they did, they would usually come to the door with a watchdog who barked at us and scared us off. Therefore, we did not make any sales there either.

After about two weeks of hardly any sales, we decided to visit the poorer residential areas. It was much easier to talk to them because most who were at home usually came to the door or asked us to come in. They were very interested in buying but had no money. So, we let them sign the sales contract and asked when we should come back. They said to return on pay day. Since a signed contract counted as a sale, we reported our sales record to Nashville and our weekly report started to show our names.

The problem came on pay day. We brought the dictionaries to each household that had signed a contract. When we rode the bus we had to load a couple of boxes on the bus. When we arrived at our territories, we unloaded the boxes, keeping them at nearby gas stations—where we begged them to store the books for a while—and with about five dictionaries in our brief cases, we knocked on the doors of signed customers. Unfortunately, most of our customers didn't have any money left from their paychecks!

I realized that I wasn't going to be successful as a salesman. To be a good salesman you have to be excited to meet people. However, I was so afraid of speaking with people. When I knocked on the door, I was already worrying about what I would say. Secondly, although Mr. Im had told us to move on to the next house once we'd sold a dictionary, I was so happy when I sold one that I ended up talking with the customer for a long time. I discovered that most people who stayed home were elderly, housewives, or unemployed people who stayed home and were in need of some company. Third, I was much more comfortable trying to sell in the poorer neighborhoods even though most of the residents did not have much money. Many of them were unemployed and therefore stayed home. But these people were so easy to talk to.

We ended up spending three and a half months of our summer trying to be salesmen without really making any money.

Enrolling in the University of Washington (1966)

We returned to Seattle and good news was waiting for me. For the fall term, Professor Worcester offered me a teaching assistant position which I gladly accepted. But I'd already committed to teach at St. Martin's College for the fall term. So, I had to teach three hours a week at UW, take my core preliminary courses (Advanced Micro and Macroeconomics plus Matrix Algebra), and teach nights at St. Martin's College.

As I began at UW, the economics department had five new assistant professors from the University of Chicago, a very conservative school in economics, with strong emphasis on monetary theory and policy. At Vanderbilt, which was a more liberal college, faculty were mostly from universities such as Harvard and MIT where monetary theory was an important subject, but not emphasized as much. These five new assistant professors were very focused on Chicago's curriculum and they almost ignored teaching us about fiscal policy. We spent most of our time learning about Milton Friedman's views on monetary policies.

There were five Koreans enrolled in the economics graduate school when I entered the Ph.D. program at UW, and none of us had a strong monetary background. Plus we all had problems with our English. After the fall term, I was just too busy, so I decided to stop teaching at St. Martin's College. Teaching there would not give me a permanent solution to settle in the U.S. I had my visa problems on my mind all the time. Also, I knew that teaching part-time would not bring me enough money to make a living.

But most importantly on my mind was that the economics department at UW had a policy that every Ph.D. student was required to take preliminary exams as soon as they finished one year's coursework. This meant that I had to study hard in preparation for those exams which I would take in the fall of 1967 or during the spring term of 1968.

A Pleasant Surprise: Reverend Dae-Sun Park Visits Seattle

One day in Seattle, I met Reverend Dae-Sun Park, the president of Yonsei University. I didn't know him personally, but when he visited Seattle, I was the one who gave him a ride from the airport to downtown Seattle. Rev. Park, who was living in Taegu, South Korea, had previously attended the very famous Pyongyang Theological Seminary. After graduating from seminary he became the pastor of West Pyongyang Methodist Church.

As we talked on our drive, I found out that he had come to the south as a refugee just like us. We started talking about our lives in Pyongyang and realized that we knew each other because he had been the pastor of the church that my mom and I had attended! Since my mother had been a deacon at the church, he remembered her and even my name.

Rev. Park asked, "Are you her son? How tragic it was that your mother stayed in Pyongyang and you went to the South when you were very young." His comment reminded me of how, despite all that I had done on my own in the U.S., my story was still a tragic and lonely one. However, it would soon change for the better as I would not be alone for much longer.

CHAPTER 7
MARRYING KUM CHOI (1967-1968)

I don't remember why I decided to get married at this point in my life when I didn't have any money, a terminal degree, or a permanent job. I didn't even have an immigrant visa to stay in the U.S. But for some reason I felt as though it was the right time in my life to get married. Looking back on my life, I now realize that marrying my wife was the best and most important turning point in my life.

Three Meetings, Then Marriage

One day in September 1967, my friend Chang Ho Hong who lived in Los Angeles asked me to come down to meet his wife's friend, Kum Choi. Mrs. Hong told me that Kum was 25 years old and worked at a computer company with her, and that she seemed like a very nice lady. So soon after that, I flew to Los Angeles for the weekend and met my future wife. We spent time together over a couple of days. When I returned to Seattle, I was busy with coursework and I really didn't have time to think of her or call her often.

One day in early 1968 my apartment mate, Mr. Koo, told me that his friend in Los Angeles was taking Kum Choi out for a date and was seriously considering proposing to her! He suggested that I should hurry to get her. I called Mrs. Hong and asked her if she knew anything about Kum's dating life, and she said that she didn't know. Since I hadn't paid too much attention to Kum after our initial meeting, Mrs. Hong thought I'd forgotten about her. I told Mrs. Hong on that call that I wanted to get serious about proposing marriage and that I would fly to Los Angeles immediately.

A few days later, Mrs. Hong called me and said that I should call Kum rather than flying to Los Angeles. Mrs. Hong also told me that Kum was a Catholic and that there was another Catholic man who was approaching her seriously. However, according to Mrs.

Hong, Kum hadn't made up her mind yet. I called Kum and told her that this time that I was serious and that I wanted to fly down to Los Angeles immediately to see her. She said that it was not necessary. So instead, we just talked and talked on the phone for about a week and we finally reached the conclusion that she would fly up to Seattle.

I proposed. She said yes. I had known her for about six months and had only met her in person three times!

We would get married during my spring break in 1968. I still don't know how or why this happened, especially when I was so busy preparing for my preliminary exams. And I was not even able to support her financially! It's still a mystery that only God can answer.

Good times in our dating days!

1984: With Elder and Mrs. Hong.

My Wife's Origins

Kum Choi was the eldest of five children born to Mr. & Mrs. Chul and Insil Choi. Her family was from Korea, but she was born on May 18, 1942 in Manchuria, in northeastern China, because her dad had moved her family there to start a business. In 1945 after the end of WWII, the Choi family moved back to Korea and lived in the Hwanghae Province, which was a southwestern province now a part of newly-created North Korea.

Apparently her dad had been successful in China making and selling *yut* (엿), a type of Korean candy made from sugar and rice.

Although they had to live under the Communist North Korean regime, they started to do well in Hwanghae Province.

But very wisely, they left their homeland together as a family and were able to move to Seoul before the Korean War started. Later during the Korean War, they had to move away from Seoul further south. They settled in Taegu for a while and later moved to Pusan, where Teresa went to elementary school. They moved back to Seoul in 1953 and Teresa went to Jim Myung High School and then graduated from Ewha Women's University. She came to America because her mother thought it was a good idea for her to go to America unless she wanted to stay in Korea and get married quickly.

1960: High school yearbook photo.   1966: Ewha University graduation.

Our Simple Seattle Wedding (April 27, 1968)

We got married on April 27, 1968 at the University Presbyterian Church on the UW campus. It was a convenient spot for our wedding because the church had a wedding coordinator who took care of everything, including the reception. It cost us $100 and that included the wedding cake! None of our parents were present at the wedding and it was strictly my wife's and my decision to marry. Finding a suitable spouse wasn't easy during my generation because most students who came from Korea were men. Only a few female students were available. Therefore, there was no time to consult with my parents, or my wife with hers, back in Korea.

1967: Our engagement party.   April 27, 1968: Our wedding day.

I heard years later from my wife's brother, Young Choi, that my mother-in-law in Seoul was so sad that her beloved first daughter was getting married to me. My mother-in-law had visited with my dad in Seoul and found out that I didn't have my real mother, that my dad had remarried a younger woman and had two children from her, and that I didn't have a permanent job or future. How could her daughter marry a man like me?

Fortunately they were in far away in Seoul and we were marrying in Seattle! Dr. Ko Byung Ik, who later became the president of Seoul National University, was a visiting professor of history at UW and served as bride's father, walking my wife-to-be down the aisle. We spent three days honeymooning in Olympic National Park. We settled in our new home on Orange Place North which was located on the top of Queen Anne Hill where we had a tremendous view of beautiful downtown Seattle.

1968: Our honeymoon in Olympic National Park.
(r) 1968: Our first apartment in Cheney, WA.

Early Years of Marriage and My First Full-Time Job

A few months later in the summer of 1968, we left Seattle so that I could take a full-time position as assistant professor of economics at Eastern Washington State College. During this period, universities and colleges were expanding their departments due to the increased enrollment of baby boomers. That increased enrollment forced schools to hire assistant professors without advanced (Ph.D.) degrees. Since I had more or less finished the coursework, they considered me a Ph.D. candidate even though I hadn't taken the preliminary exams.

We moved to Cheney, Washington and settled in a basement apartment. I felt sorry to my wife who had just married me and was hoping that I'd finish my Ph.D. at UW. But I felt the pressure to earn a living for us and so I decided that we should leave so I could get a full-time job to support us. This was probably surprising to her and something she wasn't expecting. However, she never expressed her concern or complained to me at all.

I will have more to say about my wife later, but whenever we were in a crisis, or I was in a crisis, she would never show any panic or emotion. She just took the circumstances as they came and dealt with them accordingly and as best as possible. What an amazing woman!

During this time, U.S. immigration laws changed—thanks to Robert Kennedy who sponsored the change in the U.S. Senate—to admit more immigrants. The change in the law allowed admission of professionals to the U.S., regardless of race, and allowed for people like me to apply for immigrant status since I had already earned a higher education degree which qualified me as a "professional." This law allowed many Koreans and other immigrants to come to the U.S., whereas before then very few were able to come due to immigration restrictions.

Our First Child Is Born (May 12, 1969)

Helen Hyunmee Lee was born on May 12, 1969 in Spokane, Washington at Sacred Heart Hospital. It was a good thing that I had just found a job as a teacher! To my surprise, I remember my wife crying so hard while she was recuperating in the hospital bed after delivering Helen. I asked her later why she cried so much? She said that having her first child without her mom by her side made her feel so sad, and she just couldn't stop crying. (Later on, my wife went to Helen's delivery of her first child, Jason, in Orange City, Iowa. She didn't want her daughter to deliver her first child without her mother present.)

During our time living in Cheney, we met a very nice family, Mr. and Mrs. Chaffee. They were sincere Christians and very fond of Korean immigrants. When we met them, they were already hosting a gathering at their house every Thursday evening for a group of Korean immigrants. These were mostly war brides whose husbands served at a nearby Air Force base and Mrs. Chaffee taught English to them. We were grateful to join them and it was very nice to meet some Koreans there. Two of the women who came to these gatherings were twin sisters, Jungsook and Heesook Koh, who had attended the same high school as my wife in Seoul, Korea, although they were six years younger. We became very close friends with Mrs. Chaffee and the Koh twins, and they came to our home in Cheney quite often. In fact, Mrs. Chaffee stayed with us for two weeks after Helen's birth to help with Kum's recovery. In hindsight, it is amazing to me that we were able to meet people like Mr. and Mrs. Chaffee, and many others who helped us significantly in life. I know now that none of these people were put accidentally into my life. Someone else guided us to them and them to us.

Helen was a happy camper when she was baby and a good sleeper. She was a child in the era before car seats were mandatory, so as soon as I made her a bed in the backseat of our car and tossed in new library books we'd borrowed for a camping trip, she was happily on her own in the back seat either reading or sleeping. For more than five years, we were a family of three. But it wouldn't be too much longer, though, that our family would change again, for the better.

CHAPTER 8
GRADUATING, GROWING OUR FAMILY, GOING EAST (1969-1975)

In the years to come, I continued to see evidence that God's hand was on my life and guiding me in ways that I could never have predicted. I spent three years as an assistant professor at Eastern Washington State College (EWSC), but they denied my tenure since I didn't have a Ph.D. degree. During these three years we went to Seattle during my summer vacation at EWSC, and I checked to see if I could come back to the University of Washington (UW) economics department as a full-time student so that I could take the preliminary exam for my Ph.D. However, the environment at UW was worse than when I had left. All five Koreans who had been there previously had either transferred to other universities or had just quit. I realized that my academic future had no hope at UW.

One day during my teaching at EWSC, I visited Washington State University (WSU) for a three-day economic conference. There I had a chance to visit with the graduate program director, Dr. Eldon Weeks, and the department chairman Dr. James Nelson, a Ph.D. from Harvard. As I talked with both of them, I felt that WSU might be the place where I could finish my degree. Furthermore, I had begun to realize that there was a glut of Ph.D.'s in economics, and it was getting hard for those people to find jobs. Applied economics however, like resource economics or agricultural economics, seemed to be a better path to securing employment after getting a Ph.D. degree. So I enrolled in the Ph.D. Program in agricultural and resource economics, at WSU in the fall of 1971.

With Thanks to My Dear Mentor and Friend, Walt Butcher

A Ph.D. is like having a union card--you don't know if you are going to get it until you get it! Getting a Ph.D. is dependent upon many factors such as the right timing, your dissertation chairman, how much your degree committee supports you, and so on.

When I finished my coursework, I had my thesis chairman Dr. Lee Blakeslee help me select my dissertation topic, teach me economic modeling, and help me write my outline. However, he had to leave for Thailand for an Agency for International Development (AID) project right after my proposal was accepted. So I had to find another professor as my thesis chairman. Professor Walt Butcher gladly accepted my thesis chairmanship, and what a blessing that was to me. He has been my dear mentor and friend for life!

Walt was a leading water resource economist who had just returned from his one year sabbatical teaching at the University of Wisconsin at Madison. I started writing my dissertation with his guidance. However, because he wasn't as strong in mathematical modeling, he had one condition: that he would add one additional committee member from the mathematics department who could supervise the math parts of the dissertation. Usually Ph.D. candidates have three committee members, but I would had to have four.

My dissertation topic was on how "Exogenous Changes in Energy Prices" would affect the regional (state of Washington) economy. My argument was that any region's or state's economy was affected by exogenous forces (outside forces of the region such as federal government energy policy) that affected the region's economy. During my dissertation period, we had an energy crisis in the nation and energy prices were rising. This had an enormous effect on the Washington state economy.

Energy prices were determined at the national level, and the state of Washington was a "price-taker" set by the national level, I argued. My model tried to anticipate how much an increase in energy prices would affect the regional economy.

When I was defending my dissertation at my final oral examination, my last hurdle to earning my Ph.D., was getting the approval from the committee member from the mathematics department that Walt had added. He asked me how much confidence I had that I could implement economic policies based on the numbers that I generated. I answered that I had plenty of confidence in the numbers generated for policymakers to use because they came from an empirical test based on published state of Washington Input-Output tables.

The math professor's questioning continued, however, and I hadn't expected this at my oral exam. His problem was not on the empirical studies that I had done but was more about the numbers that I had generated using a computer program. Since my calculations were input into the computer by a department programmer, I trusted that they were correct.

But even that was not the problem! The problem was that the programmer generated numbers in too much detail, for example: three more numbers after the decimal points. I used them without any modification in my dissertation. So when the value generated was in millions of dollars, the computer program generated three more values after the decimal. It read something like $567.734 million while I should have just rounded it to one decimal place at $567.7 million.

The math professor just kept asking me whether I could make a strong policy statement using thousands of dollars (three numbers after the decimal) versus using millions. He asked, "Aren't the numbers after the decimal point just "computer noise?"

In retrospect, I should have agreed with him and said that I couldn't make any meaningful policy recommendations at such a detailed level. However, since I put those detailed numbers into my dissertation I thought I had to defend the numbers!

Once I said that, I could see from his eyes that he was upset. He then started to ask me more questions about my model and the computer analyses. That was when I realized that I was in trouble. I knew one classmate had failed his final oral just one year before me. I started to get very nervous.

During this ordeal however, Walt noticed the uneasy dynamic occurring between the math professor and me. Suddenly, he left the room, explaining, "I forgot to bring a black pen to sign the paper after the oral." Later I found out that the university's regulation required committee members to sign in black ink when they passed the candidate. That signaled to the math professor that my dissertation chairman was determined to pass me at the oral. I knew that Walt had more seniority than the math professor. And what was supposed to have been about an hour oral had already taken about three hours.

When they asked me to go outside and wait for their decision, I was so nervous that I cried. I knew that I had made a big mistake at the oral and feared that all my hard work was going to go down the drain. What about my wife? My family? My future?

But after about thirty minutes Walt invited me back in. When I returned to the room he congratulated me for passing the exam! The other three members of the committee did the same. However, Walt said that he and the math professor agreed that my answer was wrong, and that I shouldn't say the numbers after the decimal point should be used to make any meaningful policy recommendation. He asked me if I agreed. This time, I said yes.

I had earned my Ph.D. Thank you, Walt. Thank you!

Professor Walt Butcher and his daughter Emily at her graduation. 1974: I became Dr. Chinkook Lee, Ph.D.

My Last Year in Washington State, And Another Child Is Born (1974)

When we were in Pullman, Washington, my wife made almost of all Helen's clothes by herself. My wife learned to sew from her mother and she was good at it. We saved lots of money with the sewing machine when we needed it the most!
When we were in Pullman, she attended kindergarten and walked about seven blocks to get to school.

I finished my Ph.D. in agricultural and resource economics at WSU in the summer of 1974, but I didn't have citizenship yet. Now that I had a terminal degree in applied economics, most of the jobs I was qualified for were in the federal or state government. Therefore, I had to wait to get my citizenship before I could get those types of jobs.

Luckily, professor Norm Whittlesey had a grant from the State of Washington to study the impact of energy cost increases on Washington State's food prices. He asked me if I would be willing to stay in Pullman as a postdoctoral research fellow. Since I had no other job offers, I decided to work with him for a year.

Our second child, Brian, was born on September 26, 1974, in Clarkston, Washington. At first we named him "Bryant" because that was the name of the street we lived on in Pullman (411 Bryant Street). But we were able later to change it to "Brian".

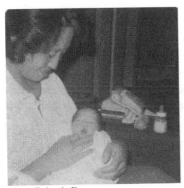
1974: Brian is Born

1975: Brian's First Birthday

Becoming an Official American (1975)

In May 1975, the district federal court in Spokane, Washington sent us a letter informing us that because our five-year legal residence in the U.S. had passed without any legal problems, we were eligible to take a citizenship test. The court asked us to bring two character witnesses for me and also for my wife. I asked Professor Butcher and his wife Elinor to be witnesses for both of us. They were glad to help, and one day we all drove about an hour and a half to travel the 70 miles from Pullman to Spokane. We were well prepared for both the oral and written citizenship tests, because we knew if we failed, we'd have to wait another six months to try again.

My wife and I went in separately. I went in first and easily passed the written test, which involved no more than writing, "I live in Pullman, Washington." Then I answered the examiner's oral questions. Everything was easy until I came to the one question I could not answer. He asked me, "When did Columbus come to America?"

I said that I hadn't seen this question covered in the citizenship preparation book. He said, "No, but since you've got a Ph.D. you should know this." He then instructed me to just guess.

I tried, "Seventeenth century?"

He said, "No! Try again!"

"Sixteenth century?"

"No!" he answered.

I started to get worried that this failure might jeopardize my citizenship. The examiner then opened my file and started to go through the final paperwork. He reached the section to finalize my legal name. I had written my name as "Chin Kook Lee" because that was what was on my Korean passport. He looked at that and said, "Now that you're going to be a U.S. citizen this is the only

60

time you have a chance to change your name without going to federal court again."

He asked me if I wanted to consider "Gene Kook Lee" since I told him that my actual name sounds more or less like "Jin" even though I wrote it as "Chin."

I immediately agreed. From that point onward, I became Gene Kook Lee, officially.

I know I didn't have to say yes, but I did it for a few reasons. First, the examiner sounded like he wanted me to change my name. Second, I was afraid of failing the exam because I couldn't answer the earlier question. When we had all finished, we returned to Pullman. My wife and I were now U.S. citizens!

On the way I asked my wife if she changed her first name. She said the examiner had asked her, but she'd said no!

I told her my story. Walt, who was driving, instantly said to me, "Oh Chin, shame on you! How could you change it to Gene? You will never be Gene." I heard Walt's dissatisfaction with my decision frequently during our hour and a half drive back to Pullman.

So my official name became "Gene," but later whenever I had to say it, listeners couldn't understand my pronunciation of "Gene." Therefore, I went back to using Chin or Chinkook, except in my legal documents, where I used "Gene K. Lee."

From Washington State to Washington, D.C.

On a Saturday afternoon in June 1975, I was out playing golf when my wife received a call from Dr. Eldon Weeks. Dr. Weeks had been the Graduate Program Director at WSU when I'd entered the program, but he had left WSU to be the chief of the Farm Income Branch in the Economic Research Service which was a part of the U.S. Department of Agriculture in Washington, D.C. On that call, he said they had a position open in his branch that fit my qualifications and that he wanted to hire me!

I returned his call and accepted. He said he'd process the paperwork through the Personnel Office and that I'd hear from them shortly. In a few weeks, he called again and told us I was hired, and that we should move to the D.C. area right away.

So in July 1975, we left Pullman for Washington, D.C., pulling a small U-Haul trailer with all of our belongings. Helen was six and Brian was ten months old. I had mixed emotions as we started the cross-country drive. It was nice finally to have a full-time job, but I wasn't certain about the place where we were headed. Would I like the job? Would my family like living in D.C.? How about my children's education? Many thoughts flooded my mind. We arrived in D.C. after driving for one week. It had taken us three days just to cross the Blue Sky state of Montana!

In her typical style, my wife never showed any concern or negative emotions about the cross-country move we were making or the uncertain life we'd be facing.

1975: On the road, heading east to Washington, D.C.

When we arrived in the D.C. area, we first lived for a year in a two-bedroom ground-level apartment in Annandale. Brian's crib was in our room, and Helen was in the second bedroom. (Helen still remembers seeing the roaches in the apartment's tiny kitchen.) Then we bought a house in Fairfax, Virginia, 5121 Pumphrey Drive. I commuted to my new job in D.C. on a Metro bus which stopped just a half block from our home. Helen and Brian went to Laurel Ridge Elementary School also just a half block away.

2017: Our granddaughter Katie outside our old house at 5121 Pumphrey Drive, Fairfax, VA. It looks much better now with a garage and an addition on the second floor!

In 1978 after we had gotten settled in the D.C. area and I had started my new job, my wife wanted to invite all of her family in Seoul to immigrate to the U.S. With the immigration restrictions removed at this time, many Koreans began taking advantage of the opportunity to invite family members to the U.S. Within a month after filing, the Immigration Office notified us that they had sent an immigration visa to her family in Seoul and that they could come to the U.S. soon. My wife's parents and her four siblings all came and decided to settle in Los Angeles.

My wife's side of the family.

It had been a fruitful decade, personally and professionally, albeit one full of big changes. But this move allowed me to begin a career that spanned nearly three decades, working for the federal government as a civil servant.

New Residents of the Washington, D.C. Metropolitan Area

CHAPTER 9
CAREER STORIES (1975-2004)

In July 1975, I reported to the Economic Research Service at the U.S. Department of Agriculture. My job at the ERS/USDA had three main components.

First, I engaged in basic research on U.S. agricultural policy. The Congress adopted U.S. farm policies every five years, passing what we called the "Farm Bill." Therefore, we knew where American farm programs were heading for the next five years which allowed us to prioritize our research and analysis.

Second, my job was to respond to inquiries from Congress, from the White House, and from the public. My job changed from time to time, but my main specialty was on aggregate economic results, such as the effect of U.S agricultural exports on the U.S. economy, in terms of employment, farm income, and food prices.

Third, my job was to keep up with professionals. In other words, the ERS/USDA was a very unique place where more than 200 Ph.D.'s in Economics worked. Therefore, our agency was tasked with keeping up with economists at universities, state and local governments, and at various agencies in the federal government. This meant we belonged to a national economic association, did professional research, and maintained relationships with other economists throughout our careers. I joined both international and national economic associations and wrote many journal articles.

Teaching part-time was also encouraged, so I also taught at various colleges during my entire career.

2017: Jim Gulley - one of my ERS colleagues and a good friend who is also a Methodist minister.
1990: With Bill Edmondson, Maureen Kinnkanin, and Gerald Schluter

Notable Highlights from my Career

Memory 1:

Twice I received calls from the White House staff through our department's regular channel. The first call was for President George H. W. Bush when he was going to Chicago to speak to a farm group on why the U.S. needed NAFTA (North American Free Trade Agreement). The other call was for President Bill Clinton when he was on his way to Dallas to promote LAFTA (Latin American Free Trade Agreement). I saw both of them in the evening news pounding the podium using sound bytes and data points that I had given to their staffers earlier that day.

Memory 2:

I did a research project that quantified how much skilled versus unskilled labor was generated from U.S. farm exports. My analyses were part of the Economic Report of the President two years in a row. This is the report that the President sends to Congress every year (usually February) right after the State of the Union speech.

Memory 3:

A couple years before my retirement, I conducted a research project on "How Much Increases in the Minimum Wage Would Affect Food Prices." President Clinton proposed increasing the minimum wage while the Republicans were against it. The legislation to increase minimum wage to $5.25 from $4.75 was debated and debated but never made it through the Republican-controlled Congress. My research conclusion was that there would be a minimal effect on food prices if the minimum wage was raised. However, as an analyst, I couldn't use the language "minimal effects" since that would help the Democrats! I had to use language that was 'politically neutral.'

During my research on the topic, Professor Alan Krueger in the department of economics at Princeton University was the leading economist on minimum wage issues. He and I met in person and had many email exchanges. He also quoted me in his speeches and publications. Years later after retiring, Professor Krueger was appointed by President Barack Obama to be Chairman of the Council of Economic Advisors at the White House.

I also spoke frequently with Dr. Jared Bernstein at the Economic Policy Institute (EPI) on the minimum wage issue. He used my publication quite a bit and also quoted me in his speeches and publications. He went on to become the chief economist for Vice President Joe Biden.

Memory 4:
In 1990, Mr. Se Hae Han, the North Korean Ambassador to the United Nations came to Washington, D.C., and I was invited to a meeting with him and about twenty other people including Mr. Richard Solomon, Assistant Secretary of State for the Far East and Pacific Islanders, North Korean specialists from the CIA, the State Department, the Korean Embassy and scholars from a few universities around D.C. Mr. Han spoke about the need for improving North Korea-U.S. relations.

Work Life as a Minority/Korean

Over the course of my time working as a minority in the federal government, I learned many hard lessons. In my early years, I noticed that it was very rare and difficult for minorities to get hired or promoted into management positions.

I also noticed that in general, there seemed to be an unwritten rule that is was good to have one minority candidate included in a review process for hiring or promoting, as if that showed that there was fairness and diversity to the process. However, I witnessed way too many highly-qualified minorities getting rejected from key management positions, time and time again.

I spent thirty years in these kinds of circumstances and I left the federal government feeling that the "race" issue will unfortunately remain in American society for a long time. I don't see how there will ever be a genuine equality among different races. However, I do think there have been many positive changes in favor of minorities and I hope that when my grandchildren grow up, they will experience less discrimination than I did over those thirty years.

Moonlighting as a College Economics Professor

During my career in the ERS/USDA, I taught part-time at night in the D.C. area mostly to supplement my income. But I also liked to teach. While I'm not a good speaker, I always enjoyed working with young economists, and I never got tired of teaching. Each new semester was always exciting. The dullest part of teaching, though, was grading, particularly distinguishing between grades. It was not easy to give someone an "A" while giving another student a "B." Flunking some students was a very hard of part of teaching.

My last teaching job was at Soka University of America in Aliso Viejo, California, just a few blocks away from our new retirement home. I was lucky to make my retirement transition from a full-time job in D.C. to teaching one year at Soka University when we arrived in Aliso Viejo.

My Wife Takes a Career Risk (1978-2003)

After we moved to D.C., my wife began working at the Export and Import Bank, a federal government agency, as an accounting technician. She started at a GS-7 (General Schedule-7) level, which meant her income wasn't very high. So she decided to look for a small business that she could own and operate. This was another turning point in our lives, and we ended up much better off financially, even though it was very hard work for my wife. I also worked hard trying to help her before and after my own job.

In 1978, we bought the Bender Building Lobby Shop from a man named Mr. Joe Nash. It was a small space, but it was a prime location inside a corner building where there was heavy traffic from both the people who were working in the building and also people who were making a shortcut through the building from either Connecticut Avenue to L Street, or vice versa.

Business was booming from the very first day. But the margins were thin, so we had to keep our costs low. My wife had to work hard each and every day, from 7 a.m. to 6 p.m., punching the cash register and standing up all day.

Due to the lobby shop business I now had three jobs: my career in ERS during regular business hours, helping my wife's business after work to free her up so she could pick up Brian at school and then go home to cook dinner for our family, and I also taught at a local community college some nights of the week. With two young kids at home it was tough, but we survived.

While she was operating the lobby shop, my wife met a very nice gentleman named Sam Rose. Mr. Rose was temporarily leasing office space in the Bender Building while his new office was being built a few blocks away. He saw my wife working hard at the lobby shop every day, and she impressed him with her strong work ethic. Therefore, after a couple of years getting acquainted, he offered us the opportunity to open a brand new restaurant/deli in prime office space near Union Station. We named it Capitol Café. Even though my wife had very little food service experience prior to this, Mr. Rose trusted that she would figure it out--and of course, she did!

We owe a great deal of thanks to Mr. Rose. After Capitol Café, he then built a brand-new larger building right next door, where the CNN Washington bureau was going to be located. And he once again graciously offered us the opportunity to open another brand new restaurant/deli there. We named that one Station Café, and my wife owned and operated that business for ten years before we finally retired.

In retrospect, had we not sold Station Café, my wife may have had the chance to work again with Sam and perhaps we could have made a lot more money. However, my wife and I both agreed that God had already given us enough money.

Also, after twenty-five years of working on her feet, managing small businesses, my wife deserved and needed a break. She had even developed a recurring cough (bronchitis) while working in the café, and we could never figure out why. Nor would it ever go away. So it was the right time to sell that business, and in 2003 we sold it and began planning for our retirement.

But before I can go further, I need to go backwards and tell the story of how in the midst of our time in Washington, D.C., I discovered that my mother was still alive in North Korea!

CHAPTER 10
LOOKING FOR MY MOTHER IN NORTH KOREA
(1983, 1987, 1989)

In 1983, I decided to send an inquiry letter about my mother to the North Korean embassy in Beijing. President Jimmy Carter had relaxed the ban on Americans visiting Communist countries such as North Korea, Cuba, and Libya. Therefore, it was possible to visit Pyongyang if I acquired an entry visa.

There was no immediate reply from the embassy, but I had heard from many others who had sent the same type of letter that it took a few years to get a reply. I continued to write to the embassy consistently and also asked any friends I knew who were going to visit Pyongyang to inquire about my mother's' whereabouts. In 1987, I received an unofficial answer from a friend of mine, Dr. Yang Eun Sik, who somehow determined that my mother had died a long time ago. I gave up searching for my mother after I heard this news.

A Surprise in the Summer of 1989

Then in the summer of 1989, my wife and I were just returning from a visit to Seoul. We were stopping over in Los Angeles to visit family when we got an unexpected call. My friend, Rev. Eun Hong Kang, was in Tokyo and had called our home in D.C. during Helen's summer break from college, so she had been trying to contact us. Rev. Kang had found out that my mother was still alive!

When we returned to D.C., Rev. Kang told me that the North Korean government had issued me a visa and that I should plan to go to Pyongyang immediately to see my mother. But I couldn't make my trip right away because I had a teaching commitment at the USDA Graduate School for the fall 1989 quarter. My night school class started right after Labor Day and ended the second week of December. So I made plans to leave for Pyongyang as soon as the school quarter was over.

I could hardly believe that my mother was alive and that I had plans to finally see her again for the first time in 39 years!

It was December 10, 1989. My whole family came to Dulles airport to give me a bon voyage sendoff. I would fly through Beijing before taking another flight to Pyongyang. It was a very foggy morning when I arrived in Beijing, and a diplomat from the North Korean embassy was waiting for me at the airport. He took me to a Chinese hotel, Il-Dan, that was close to the North Korean embassy.

The diplomat said that it would take a couple of days to get a visa and suggested I take a tour to the Great Wall and Tiananmen Square while I waited for the visa, which I did. After a couple of days, the North Korean diplomat came to my hotel and said I would be leaving Beijing for Pyongyang the following day.

The plane carrying us, Choson Airline, had engine trouble and we had to make an emergency landing at Sanyang (Bongchun) in northwest China. After a five-hour delay, we departed again and finally arrived at the Pyongyang airport where three North Korean agents greeted me: a driver, a tour guide for Korean-Americans visiting Pyongyang, and a officer from the Committee on Fatherland Unification (which is similar to the CIA).

During the plane ride I had so many thoughts about my mother. The last time I saw her was in 1950 when I had said, "See you next week." I was nearly thirteen when I left my mother and I was coming home to see her thirty-nine years later, as a fifty-two year old! All I could remember was that my mother was a Christian and took me to Sunday school. I couldn't even remember well what my mother looked like! I worried that even if they brought a fake mother, I probably wouldn't be able to recognize her as being fake.

After I got through the immigration process, I was taken to a VIP waiting room. My mother's brother was there waiting for me. I recognized him right away. My heart was beating quickly because I was expecting to finally see my mother at long last. I asked him, "How come mom didn't come to the airport, is she sick?" He didn't answer my question.

But after I had settled down in a chair, he told me that my mother had died of heart attack only a few months earlier.

What an unexpected and sad surprise. I had come all the way to Pyongyang from D.C. with so much anticipation about seeing my mother and then heard that my mother was dead. I couldn't believe it. We drove to Koryo Hotel, and I was able to sit down with my uncle to hear the details of my mother's death. I videotaped his explanation.

She'd had heart problems and apparently died of a heart attack after hearing that I was coming home to see her.

October 1989 is when she passed. My uncle said there hadn't been any communication that I was coming until the first week of December. By then, it was too late to let me know before leaving D.C.

Somehow I didn't cry at the beginning. At the Koryo hotel, I made a call to my wife and told her the sad story, asking her to relay it to my brother in Seoul. The next morning I told the agent that I wanted to shorten my two-week stay in order to leave in a week. I was only interested in visiting my mom's tomb.

I never cried more in my life than when I visited my mother's tomb. It was located on a hill, way up a rural mountain in Pyong Ahn Nam-do province. When I saw the name of the tomb-owner written on the back of tombstone, I cried and cried and cried. Why were the owners of my mother's tomb not my brother and me?!?!?!!!

The guide said, "Mr. Lee, I can understand your sadness and I want you cry as much as you want. We'll wait for you until you settle down." I cried so loud and so long!

Back to D.C.

Before I left Pyongyang, I sat down with all the relatives who remained and asked them how my mother lived. They said that after we left, she and our grandma lived together, expecting that we'd return home soon. There were lots of ups and downs, and she didn't have a job at the time. So she worked here and there for a few years and then our grandma died, leaving my mother alone.

I heard that she, who was a strong Christian when I left her, had become a devoted Communist. I'm sure that my mother did not want to be a Communist, but the environment had caused it. Apparently she had to do it to survive. That is so very sad.
She had lived in a remote rural area, and we went there on the third day of my visit. She had lived with my cousin (my dad's brother's daughter), so we visited my cousin's house. There they showed me my mother's picture that was a few years old. Of course I couldn't recognize her as my mother! I had to take their word for it.

I left Pyongyang on a snowy day and returned back to Dulles Airport outside of Washington, D.C. My wife and my kids were there waiting for me. I embraced all of them and we cried and cried at the airport. It had been a snowy day when we'd arrived in Seoul, from Pyongyang, on my thirteenth birthday in 1950, and the snow at the Dulles airport that day somehow brought me back to that sadness.

At that moment, I felt that life was so meaningless. Even with my wife and two kids embracing me right then and there, I felt so empty. How could my dream to see my mother vanish after I made such a long and eagerly-sought trip?

Returning to Pyongyang With My Wife (1991)

In 1991, I had to attend a work meeting in Tokyo and also another meeting in Yun Byun (연변) in the northeastern part of China, and my wife came with me. The government paid for my trip to Tokyo. The meeting in Yun Byun was the 3rd meeting of Korean Chinese, Korean Japanese, Korean American, Korean European, and South and North Koreans on Korean issues. I planned to present a paper and also was carrying scholarship funds to a student in Yun Byun from the Korean American Scholarship Foundation in D.C.

After the Tokyo meeting, we flew to Beijing and stayed a few days to sightsee. Our plan was to book airline reservations to Yun Byun when we got to Beijing. However, they were all sold out. The train from Beijing to Yun Byun could take five days. So we gave up our planned trip to Yun Byun. But this created an opportunity for us, so we decided to check with the North Korean embassy to see if they were willing to issue us a visa to visit Pyongyang.

The same North Korean diplomat who helped me get the visa in 1989 was still working in the embassy. He said he would check with the office in Pyongyang and would get back to me at our hotel. After a few days he came to the hotel with the visa and we were allowed to join a church group from San Francisco that was going to visit Pyongyang and tour the Diamond Mountain in the southeastern part of North Korea.

Upon arrival, my wife and I went straight to visit my mother's tomb. It was my second time visiting my mother's tomb and I was glad to be back with my emotions in check. This time I felt like I truly was able to pay my respects to and honor her.

1991: Visiting my mother's grave. Between Kum and I are my cousin (my dad's stepbrother's daughter), and her family.

We stayed one night at my aunt's house and returned to Pyongyang the next day. On that evening, I met Mr. See Hae Han in the hotel lobby; he was the North Korean ambassador to the UN in New York. I'd met him in 1990 in D.C. when he came to a meeting with North Korean specialists from the CIA, the State Department, the Korean Embassy, and local universities.

For some reason, Mr. Han asked me if I knew the time difference to Atlanta. Since my wife had been trying to call my daughter in D.C., she knew that it was about nine in the morning in Atlanta. Later I found out that he was calling former President Jimmy Carter to invite him to Pyongyang. I do think that President Carter eventually came to Pyongyang and met with Kim Il Sung.

After our trip to North Korea, we visited my dad and brother in Seoul, and I brought a few of my mother's pictures that I had gotten from Pyongyang. When I showed them to my dad, he claimed that the pictures were not my mother! He insisted that Communists in the North had made fake pictures for me.

I had a hard time explaining to my dad that I received the pictures from my cousin, with whom my mom lived for years, and they were real. Finally my brother, who had better memories of our mom than my dad's memory of his wife, got mad at our dad and explained to him that those pictures were indeed of his wife. Eventually my dad calmed down.

Visiting Communist North Korea as a U.S. Citizen

Even though President Carter relaxed the ban on Americans visiting terrorist countries— such as North Korea, Libya, and Cuba—making it legal to visit those countries as an American, I still reported my trip to Pyongyang to my office supervisor at the ERS/USDA even though I wasn't required to.

Before I traveled there the first time in 1989, my supervisor had reported my desire to make a trip to Pyongyang, and I ended up visiting with our security agent in the USDA who was more or less from the CIA. He gave me some advice on things to do and not to do while in Pyongyang. First, he said I should not take any message from anyone in the U.S. to North Korea. Second, he advised me to remember that I'm going as a citizen, not as a U.S. government official. Third, he ordered me to debrief him upon my return. Fourth, because the U.S. has no diplomatic ties with North Korea, he said there was likely no way the U.S. government could rescue me if North Korea decided to keep me in Pyongyang as a hostage. However, he said that in such a case I should ask to talk to the Embassy of Sweden. He said that the Swedish embassy was acting as a liaison on behalf of the U.S. in Pyongyang.

The last thing he said was pretty memorable. He said that if I became desperate in Pyongyang, because they had decided to keep me there as a hostage, I should use "common sense" to get out of North Korea. He said that in some cases they might demand that someone denounce the U.S. and its foreign policy.

"So say and do whatever you need to do to get out of there," he said. "The most important thing is that you get out of there. If you do, we will trust your word over theirs and we'll take care of you when you get out. But we can't take care of you if you're stuck in North Korea."

When I returned home, I went to see this USDA security officer and he debriefed me. I told him my sad story about not seeing my mother. A couple of months later I got a call from one of my colleagues who said that there was a man from the CIA who was doing research on North Korean agriculture and wanted to visit with me. I met with him a few times, and I also gave him my draft of a paper on North Korean agriculture that I wrote detailing what I observed when I visited there.

That CIA agent and I had a few meetings and he also kindly gave me his comments to my paper. One day he called me and asked me to have lunch. He told me that he was leaving the CIA office in Langley, Virginia, and would be transferring to the U.S. embassy in Japan.

A couple of months later, I received another call from a colleague in the ERS saying that there was another CIA agent, who had a Ph.D. from Pittsburgh, who wanted to see me. We had lunch together and he said he was taking over for the previous agent and focusing on North Korean agriculture. We met a couple of times and at our last meeting he gave me a Korean Map that included North Korea as a souvenir. He said this map was made by the CIA.

I hung the CIA map of North Korea on my office wall and kept it until I retired. Many times I jokingly told my colleagues to be careful what they are saying because the map might have a bug that listens to our conversations.

Additional Korean War Stories and Tragedies

Mine is not the only tragic story that resulted from the Korean War. There were numerous other sad situations, which illustrate how horrible war can be with effects that live on and on.

The Struggle of North Korean Pastors Who Cannot Return

There was a big problem among pastors born in North Korea who had come to the South alone, leaving their wives at home thinking they'd return within a week. That tragic thinking also resulted in most pastors who had been born in North Korea living in limbo and confusion about whether or not to remarry.

Eventually most ministers remarried while some did not. However many of those who remarried wrestled with emotional agony as they stood at the podium to preach. I saw and heard many of them crying as they preached and openly asked for God's forgiveness.

My pastor in Taegu, Kee Young Kim, was one of those who did not remarry and was very adamant that married North Korean pastors should not remarry in the South. He later immigrated to Los Angeles and became the pastor of Young Nak Presbyterian Church in Los Angeles, one of the largest Korean churches in the U.S.

Later in life, he also visited North Korea about a year after me. On his trip, he was reunited with his wife who still lived in the North and who he had left behind forty-two years prior. But to his surprise, Rev. Kim found out that his wife had remarried in the

North and also had a son who was already grown up. He was so astonished by the news that it was reported in the media that he had a heart attack while visiting his wife and homeland.

Married Man Remarries and Later Reunites With His First Wife

When my wife and I visited Pyongyang in 1991, there was a gentleman who was about ten years older than me who sat in front of us on one of tour bus rides. He was holding the hand of a lady who apparently was his wife, but during the Korean War he had left her alone to go to the South. She was crying just like I cried when visiting my mother's grave, and just like many other war-torn Korean family members have cried.

In 1950, this man had left North Korea right after they were married and she was pregnant. Many years later, he had immigrated to the U.S., moved to San Francisco and then eventually remarried. His new wife at some point suggested that he should visit North Korea and try and reunite with his original wife, if she was still alive.

He discovered that she still was alive and had never remarried, and their son was born soon after he left. Now he had finally reunited with his first wife and his son! But she kept crying because she knew she had to say goodbye to her husband a few days later and then she would be left all alone with her son. She had kept the wedding ring and showed it to us while she was crying.

At the end of the trip the man left with his group to return to San Francisco, and I can't even describe the anguishing scene when they parted. What a sad story!

My Dad Never Getting Back to His Homeland

My dad, who died in 1998 in Seoul, repeatedly told us that he wanted to return to his homeland before he died. He wanted to see with his own eyes our mother's tomb and also talk to those relatives about how my mother had lived and died. It is sad that he passed away without receiving his wish.

Also, isn't it sad that my mother was buried in Pyongyang in 1989; my father was buried in Seoul in 1998; my elder brother was buried in Auckland, New Zealand in 2012, and finally, I probably will be laid to rest somewhere in the United States?

What a tragedy of war that each member of our family will be buried in different countries! And what is worse, this is not a unique story. I had always hoped that there would be more political/social efforts to help Korean families impacted by the war reunify with their families in the North or perhaps participate in family visit programs. Now that my generation is growing older and passing away, these reunifications may never occur. I hope the next generation will at least be able to gather these stories so they can honor the memories of those who never received their wishes to unify with their loved ones.

CHAPTER 11
THE MYSTERY OF FAITH

I owe my faith to my mother. Even though I lost her, even though she would not be there for most of my life, I am eternally grateful that she shared the Christian life with me and set an example of what it looks like to be a devoted Christian.

I am also blessed that my faith grew the most when I was at Keisung High School in Taegu. This was a very difficult period of my life, and looking back I know that I survived all of those personal, family, and other hardships because my faith kept me strong and focused on what really mattered.

Ironically, when I went to Seoul to go to Soongsil, which was a Christian school, my faith weakened due to distractions and my disappointment in not getting into SNU. But when I came to U.S., my faith grew slowly but steadily, albeit with some bumps in the road. And I now see how it was all part of God's plan for me.

Korean Immigrant Church Experiences

I attended church in Los Angeles with Chang Ho Hong, my close friend who later introduced me to my future wife. Most Korean immigrants in the U.S. gathered in church during the weekend to both worship and socialize. I continued to attend church in Nashville, Seattle, Cheney/Pullman, and in D.C.

In D.C., we briefly attended the oldest Korean church in the city, Washington Korean Methodist Church. Then we met Rev. Choong Ho Huh, who also had been at Soongsil and was also a refugee from North Korea. We attended his church, First Korean Presbyterian Church in College Park, Maryland, even though it was an hour's drive away. Then when we moved to Bethesda, we attended a church nearby, United Korean Presbyterian Church.

We hoped this was the church we could settle into for the long-term. Both Helen and Brian attended Sunday school regularly and even Saturday Korean language school for a brief time. However, the problem with many Korean immigrant churches is that they are not used to working together in a constructive manner. They seemed to have difficulty avoiding infighting and power struggles in matters such as electing elders. Disagreements between the pastor and elders also seemed to happen frequently.

One time when I came home from a trip overseas, I learned that our church was about to split. Since I was not really involved in church affairs and didn't know what was going on, I couldn't decide which side to go with. Therefore, we ended up not going to church for a while.

But soon my wife and I decided to join Rockville Korean Presbyterian Church, which was one of the new churches created when our other church split. Unfortunately that church experienced many of the same issues as our previous church, and it ultimately split as well.

Eventually we ended up going back to our previous church in Bethesda, joining the congregation that had not split off. But that church again had similar problems again and its congregation got smaller and smaller over time. So over time we attended less and less frequently.

The Mystery of Faith: Becoming Catholic (2003)

In part due to all these problems in Korean Protestant churches, and also because my wife longed to go back to the Catholic tradition, I ended up becoming Catholic in 2003.

2003: Father Paul Lee presided at my baptism.
2009: With my godfather, Matthew Lee, and his wife Katherine - Portland, Maine.

During the summer of 2003, I wrote an article in Korean for our church magazine titled "The Mystery of Faith" which tells my story. Some excerpts appear below:

> *In every human being's life there are many events that don't occur the way one wants. No matter how hard you try, and no matter how thoughtfully you think about them, things that can go wrong will go wrong, while things can go right will go right unexpectedly.*
>
> *When I review my entire life, I can see that there were many things that I wanted to accomplish that I ended up not accomplishing and there were also many things I accomplished that I didn't expect. For example, I still think it is a mystery that I worked at the federal government for over thirty years. How did I end up working at the U.S. government near the White House? I never dreamed of that and never planned to do it when I came to this country. My plan was to go back home as soon as I finished my education in the U.S. But time has passed and I'm now preparing for my retirement from the U.S. government. What unexpected changes in my life! Do circumstances or environment control my destiny?*
>
> *Human beings have certain goals during their lives and work hard to accomplish them. However, it isn't easy to fulfill those goals. Like many others, I had a dream to achieve certain things. For example, I wanted to be a successful businessman making lots of money when I was a young man. That's why I entered the College of Commerce and majored in Economics. When I review my past, however, I realize that my mind wasn't set on making money. I wasn't a risk-taker. I was a very narrow-minded person worrying about small things. And,*

I now know that you can't be a successful businessman with such a mindset. Therefore, I failed to achieve that goal.

My faith is another facet of my life that isn't going the way I wanted it to. Isn't faith what you believe in and act upon? I have to confess that I'd never thought about becoming a Catholic during most of my life. However in fact, I became a Catholic on Easter of 2003.

This is a mystery to me. I spent almost all of my life as a Protestant, more specifically as a Presbyterian. I finished high school in Taegu at Presbyterian Boys' Academy and finished college at Soongsil University (Union Christian College) which was established by American Presbyterian missionaries. Then, how could I end up becoming a Catholic? I just don't know. However, I know that I didn't become a Catholic because I know the clear differences between old church (catholic) and new church (protestant). Neither had I become Catholic because my faith would grow better as a Catholic. It is a mystery and my circumstances led me to be a Catholic.

I have to confess that my Christian life got tangled up with many unfortunate church-related events, particularly conflicts that occurred between pastors and elders in my previous churches. Therefore, I ended up not going to church for a while. On Sundays, I was mostly gone to play golf.

My wife, whose faith is stronger than mine, missed not having a strong church as a key part of her life, and she finally decided to attend Catholic mass. My wife was from a Catholic family and she became a Protestant (Presbyterian) when she married me.

While I was often at golf courses on Sundays, I had an empty feeling in my mind not going to church, and it was particularly obvious to me on Easter and Christmas Sundays. I think that this empty feeling was coming from my basic faith that I inherited from my mother, my high school years, and also attending churches in America.

Therefore, starting in 2000 I slowly started to attend Sunday Mass with my wife, and eventually I became a Catholic on Easter Sunday, 2003. My mother-in-law, who was a very devout Catholic, came from

Los Angeles to witness my conversion. Both of my children were there too.

During the year-long training period to be a Catholic, I had a chance to read many religious books. The first one was a biography by a Presbyterian pastor who retired after serving almost sixty years. He was trained as a lawyer and also as a pastor. He served in Chicago at the United Korean Presbyterian Church almost entire his life. He was also a refugee, like me, from North Korea. After retiring from the Korean Church in Chicago he was called upon to continue his service at the Young Nak Presbyterian Church in Seoul, the largest Presbyterian Church in Korea. His memoir, Over the Mountain Cross the River, was written right after his retirement from Young Nak Church and was published by the Center of Asian Studies, Western Washington University in Bellingham, in 2000. In his book, he concludes by saying:

> *"I believe there is God behind every movement of Human Beings. Human Beings can't see Him nor is He known to us but He controls our lives. While our history is being made, He puts us in a special environment and controls us which many human beings do not recognize this powerful force. However, when we finish our lives and look back we know that someone else controlled our life than us doing it by ourselves. Sometimes, I walked through some dark points of my life but I still know that God controlled my life."*

Another book that I read was Father Avery Dulles' book, The Assurance of Things Hoped For (Oxford University Press, 1994). Father Dulles was just promoted to be a Cardinal by Pope Paul on February 21, 2004. Father Dulles quotes Chapter 2, verses 14-26 of the book of James to argue that "faith without practice is no faith."

> *"What does it profit, my brethren, if a man says he has faith but has not works? Can his faith save him? If a brother or sister is ill-clad and in lack of daily food and one of you says to them, Go in peace, be warmed and filled, without giving them the things needed for the body, what*

does it profit? So, faith by itself, if it has no works is dead."

I also learned that this was the fundamental difference between Catholics and Protestants from Deacon Uhm's lecture when he taught us in the training session. Deacon Uhm said that "believing" Christ as the Son of God is good enough to be saved as a Protestant but in Catholicism, you have to act like Christian: believing alone is not enough to be saved.

Father Dulles continues in his book that "faith is itself a mystery and you have to show by your practice of faith. Faith is not coming from us but comes from the grace of God. Therefore, the mystery of God is infinite which human beings can't understand with our limited mind. We have to understand that we can't understand God's mystery of grace by faith, but we have to believe in it."

An interesting part of Father Dulles' history is that he was born in a traditional Presbyterian family but was an atheist until he graduated from Harvard. While he was denying God, his grandfather was a professor of theology at a Presbyterian theology, and all his family were members of a Presbyterian Church.

When he returned from World War II, somehow he decided to convert to Catholicism. I couldn't discover why he became a Catholic in his book.

However, isn't it a mystery of faith that Father Dulles, who believed there was no God, became a cardinal?

A third book that I read was Hyun-Gak's Mahn-Haeng (만행). Hyun-Gak grew up in a strict Catholic family and later followed Buddhism. Although he became a monk he claimed he still had Christian faith. He said that he followed Buddhist teaching to follow Jesus Christ with more discipline, through meditation and by rejecting social sins.

While I was reading his book, I was impressed by his humble statement, "I meditate to be a good human being because I don't know." He said that we have to be humble and approach life with an attitude of "I only don't know" and thus ask for God's guidance.

I Corinthians 3:7 explains, "So neither he who plants nor he who waters is anything, but only God who gives the growth."

As I enter Mass each Sunday, I pray and ask God to please lead me and make my faith grow.

Oh, mystery of faith!

CHAPTER 12
FAMILY AND FRIENDS

Our Kids Through the Years

Our children experienced life as the children of immigrants (the "second generation") and went through some tough times as they were growing up. Since my wife and I both worked, we had to leave them home alone during the workweek way earlier than would be allowed today. I confess that I didn't do a good job being an involved father. My wife always wanted to be a good housewife and stay home with the children. However, the reality of our life meant I wasn't able to accommodate her wish. Financially, we couldn't support it.

When we moved to Annandale, Virginia, Helen skipped one grade because she already knew how to read, write and do math as well and started her new school in a blended second/third grade classroom. A year later, we moved to Fairfax, Virginia.

Helen shouldered many of the responsibilities when we lived on Pumphrey Drive in Fairfax. Since my wife and I worked, she had to take care of Brian, feeding, clothing, and sending him off to school which was a block away. For her last two years of elementary school in fifth and sixth grade, Helen commuted to a gifted school which was a thirty-minute drive away. I didn't realize it then, but Helen didn't like that school at all. She still remembers one teacher there who asked Helen to identify herself as a "non-white" student as a class activity in which everyone else in the class was white. When we moved to Bethesda, Maryland, Helen continued to take care of Brian.

Brian also grew up having to take care of himself during the workweek. It probably wasn't easy for him to wake up early every morning and get dressed, eat, pack his backpack, and go to school. He did it all by himself, occasionally with Helen's help.

Our home for twelve years: 8204 Bryant Drive, Bethesda, MD

In 1980, we moved to Bethesda, Maryland, Helen finished high school there and went to Williams College, a prestigious, small liberal-arts college in western Massachusetts. I had never heard of this school when Helen said she wanted to attend, but now it's one of my favorite places to visit and play golf at the lovely Taconic Golf Club.

In 1991, we moved to Potomac, Maryland, fortunate to be able to buy a home we loved, when Brian was still in high school. In 1992 after graduating, Brian also went to Williams College.

10217 Holly Hill Place, Potomac, MD

As the kids grew older, they each had their own areas of interest and skill. Helen participated in Walt Whitman High School's newspaper as a writer and editor. Those jobs took up a great deal of her time. She already demonstrated then that she was a good writer. Brian was more involved with athletics. He played soccer in elementary school, tennis in junior high, and then golf in high school. At Williams, he was captain of the varsity golf team.

Helen grew in the Christian faith early in her life, beginning at Fairfax Baptist Temple which she attended by herself at first when she was only 6! She would ride the big blue bus that picked up all the other kids in the Annandale apartment complex where we lived to go to this church every Sunday. Brian missed the chance to grow in his faith early in his life because so many of the Korean churches we attended when he was a child split up which affected his views on Christianity. He also missed the opportunity to get baptized early in his life, but later would do so in 2007.

Helen stayed at Williams as an Intervarsity Christian Fellowship campus staff worker for two years after graduation, then later became an assistant editor of Christianity Today. She has written two flagship articles about the Asian American church for this magazine, one in 1996 ("Silent Exodus: Can the East Asian Church reverse the flight of its next generation?") and a redux in 2014 ("Silent No More: Asian American Christians are growing in influence and audience. Will they be embraced by their broader church family?") She is now working at InterVarsity Press, the book publishing division of InterVarsity Christian Fellowship. Brian after graduation went to work in investment banking and then in private equity.

Their mom was always good to them, but I don't know that I was a good dad. However, I'm glad that our two children grew up without giving us too much trouble and were good children. We are very fortunate. Sometimes, I wonder how they grew to be such nice children when we didn't have enough time to take care of them, particularly me! I certainly hope our grandchildren will be the same way to their parents, as their parents were to us, when they grow up.

Our Family Has Never Missed a Thanksgiving Together...

Our family's Thanksgiving traditions began when our children were still at home but became even more meaningful when they returned home from college for Thanksgiving holidays.

We started this tradition due to our experience at Pullman. When I was a postdoc, professor Norm Whittlesey invited us (just three of us then: me, my wife, and Helen) to their home one Thanksgiving day. We went to their house about two o'clock, started drinking homemade wine, watched NFL football, and ate Thanksgiving dinner together around four o'clock. As we all sat and prayed before eating the turkey, there were three deer passing by their dining room windows. It was a snowy day and my wife and I never forgot that memory, nor that day, which is why we started our own family traditions on this annual holiday.

My Life Without Too Many Close Friends

My wife has many good friends around the world from her high school and college years and thereafter with whom she still stays in touch. However, I'm sad to say that I don't have many "close" friends. I don't know how this happened to me, but at this stage of my life, I'm realizing this is a sad fact. My wife always said to me that I needed to find some more close friends and not doing that was my fault. Perhaps this happened because I'm a very isolated person?

When I lived in Taegu, most students in that middle high school were from North Korea, just like me. So we came to school to study but we had to go to work right after classes to make a living. So there were no afterschool programs for students to get together with classmates and I did not have many friends. Then at Keisung High School, I did actually have some good friends, particularly my classmates who attended the same church as I did. I still have some contact with them.

However, I was also lonesome in Keisung High because most of my classmates were born in Taegu and I was one of only a few from North Korea. We had different speech dialects and many of my classmates teased me for my accent. They didn't realize how terrible the war was because they didn't experience it as I did.

At Soongsil, most students left school as soon as classes were finished. There weren't many extracurricular activities there either. The college was also located far away from the center of Seoul and it was hard to get together with and get acquainted with my classmates.

In the U.S., I met some good friends at Vanderbilt, but it was a very short time to get to know each other and we struggled to stay in touch.

I had a few friends in Seattle with whom I still have close contact. I also made some friends while I was in Cheney and in Pullman with whom we're still in touch!

My years in Washington D.C. also gave me the opportunity to find some good friends who shared common interests with me, like golf or economics. In hindsight, I probably could have made more good friends if I'd stayed in one church for a long time, but that didn't happen.

My years in the government as a researcher more or less allowed me to isolate myself in my office, and I always felt more comfortable staying isolated and doing things by myself. Occasional conversation with colleagues and meetings were my only contact with others. Furthermore, my wife always reminded me that "giving is more blessed than receiving." She said "yes" most of the time to her friends, even when it was a hardship for her. I didn't make those sacrifices, and I realize now that perhaps I'm too self-centered to make good friends!

Perhaps due to temperament and personality, perhaps due to life circumstance, I lived my whole life without too many close friends. Sometimes I feel sad about this, and yet at the same time that is just the way I turned out. That said, I hope that my children and grandchildren don't follow in my footsteps in this regard.

CHAPTER 13
RETIREMENT AND NEW BEGINNINGS
(2004-PRESENT)

Many people do not retire as soon as I did or never retire at all. So why did I do it?

My wife may not even know this, but the main reason for my retirement was that I wanted to spend a few enjoyable years with her! She worked so hard her whole life and didn't really have much time to enjoy herself or for us to enjoy things together. I figured that my full retirement benefits from the government and her SEP (Self Employed Program) retirement funds from her businesses would give us just enough income to live without worrying too much financially. So as soon as we reached that point, I was ready to retire.

We wanted to move to an area where the weather was favorable for retirees. My wife doesn't like cold places and always wanted to live in a warm place. I also wanted to move to California where I started my American life. It turned out that Aliso Viejo is one of the world's two best places to live—the other is Costa Del Sol in Spain. At least that's what people in this area say and now we believe it!

I also decided that I had lived enough of my life at the world's political center. Daily news from D.C. that deals with world politics was the last thing I wanted to hear everyday after my retirement!

One positive aspect of our retirement in California is that my wife's bronchitis/coughing problem has largely disappeared. No more coughing that our two children and I were so worried about!

From East Coast to Southern California (August 2004)

On August 4, 2004, our journey to retired life started as we left DC and started a cross-country drive.

Many friends warned us that it wasn't a good move. They said that we shouldn't leave friends and the area where we'd spent more than thirty years of our lives. However, ever since I'd left home in Pyongyang, no place really felt like "home." And Southern California was the place where I'd started my American life in the early 1960s. My wife's mom and brothers were also there, so she was also happy to move. And we were looking forward to leaving behind cold weather for good!

Our first stop was at our son's place in lower Manhattan, New York. We had dinner with him and stayed overnight at his apartment. The next day we drove to Binghamton, New York where my hometown friend Rev. Edwin Kang lived. He had retired from the Presbyterian Church-U.S.A and lived in the Presbyterian ministers' retirement home. We spent a day with him there, and he took us to a Korean restaurant for a good dinner. From Binghamton, we proceeded north to Kingston, Ontario, in Canada, where we met Mr. & Mrs. In-ho Uhm. They came down from Ottawa to Kingston to meet us. We had dinner and an enjoyable conversation with them.

The next day we drove to Toronto where Helen's in-laws Mr. & Mrs. Sam Lee live. We stayed there for a couple of days and proceeded further north to the town of Weldington. Brian's dad graciously arranged for us to play golf in Toronto. After an overnight stay, we drove along Canadian Highway 1 to Sault Ste Marie to meet Dr. and Mrs. Jong Sue You. Dr. You had taught economics with me at Eastern Washington State College.

After two days in Sault Ste Marie, we drove south, crossing the bridge bordering the U.S. and Canada. From there we drove to Bayshore, Wisconsin, at the southern tip of Lake Superior. It was a beautiful bay where vacationers came, and we couldn't find any motel or hotel for the extra day we wanted to spend. The next day we drove to Fargo, North Dakota, where we spent a couple days with Professor Koo, a friend of mine who was a professor at North Dakota State University. From Fargo we drove about 800 miles in one day to reach Mt. Rushmore in South Dakota. The next day we drove through Montana and stayed overnight in Butte,

Montana. From Butte we drove past Kellogg, Idaho to Coeur d'Alene, Idaho.

Kellogg is the place where our former friends Mr. and Mrs. Richard and Pat Uhm lived in the late 60s and 70s. When I was teaching at EWSC, we often visited them during the weekends and they also visited us in Spokane.

We spent one day there and the next morning we arrived in Spokane, Washington, where our daughter Helen was born. Spokane hadn't changed much over the previous thirty years. We stopped in downtown Spokane for a Starbucks coffee and reflected on our life in Spokane. Then we drove to Cheney where I started my teaching career. The apartment we lived in and the grocery store where we used to shop were still there. We noticed that other than few new buildings, not much had changed in Cheney, either.

The next day, we drove to Bellingham, Washington, to visit my former professor at Washington State University, Dr. Lee Blakeslee and his wife Yoshie. We spent two nights at their house talking about our lives in Pullman and also played two rounds of golf on the foothills of the beautiful Whitman Mountain.

Our next stop was in Seattle, Washington, where our friends during our early married life, Mr. and Mrs. Ick Whan Lee were waiting for us. We spent a day with them and he also invited Mr. & Mrs. Kie Ryun Lee to dinner. We talked about our life in the late 60s in Seattle. We also met some WSU-graduate Korean friends the next day before leaving for Oregon.

Brian recommended that we spend a day or so in Bandon Dunes, Oregon, where some new world class golf courses were located. They had two courses and so we played two rounds. The only problem was they were modeled after Scotland's link courses: both courses were hilly, windy and no carts were allowed. My knee was hurting but it was worth it to play such beautiful courses right on the Pacific Ocean.

We drove to northern California after that and visited Shasta Mountain Resorts. From there we headed to San Francisco to rest for a day at the home of Dr. and Mrs. Tae Young and Hasook Yum. From San Francisco we drove the Pacific Coast Highway to Hearst Cattle and to Santa Barbara. We also spent a couple of hours in Ojai, California, where we once considered retiring.

We arrived in Aliso Viejo, California, at about 3 pm on August 27, 2004. As soon as we unloaded our belongings, we went to Koo-Wol-San restaurant in Irvine to rendezvous with Father Paul Lee, his brother Matt Lee, and others for dinner.

Our Retired Life in Southern California

Our retired life started in Aliso Viejo in 2004. Actually, for me it started in 2005 since I taught one year at Soka University as a part-time instructor in economics. It's a great place to retire for those who love outdoor activities. Since we enjoy golf, my wife and I joined Dove Canyon Country Club and as part of our retired life routine we began playing golf four days a week.

Our retirement home: 49 Southern Hills Drive, Aliso Viejo, CA
Dove Canyon Country Club with our retired Korean friends.

Since I started my American life in Los Angeles, I felt nostalgic about the city. The place where my mother-in-law used to live before she passed away is only a few blocks away from where I started my American life. Therefore, whenever my wife and I visited my mother-in-law, I would tell her to spend some time with her mother at her apartment so I could drive around the place where I started. The houses in that neighborhood are now very old and the area is filled with mostly Hispanic people now and a few University of Southern California-owned student housing buildings. Whenever I go there I ponder how I ended up coming to the Los Angeles area after retiring and how in the world my-mother-in-law lived just a few blocks away from the place where I started my American life!

The Joy of Our Grandchildren (2002, 2005, 2007, 2008, 2010)

On July 27, 2002, our first grandchild Jason Minju Lee was born in Orange City, Iowa, a farm-filled rural small city where our son-in-law, Brian H., was working as professor at Northwestern College.

I didn't really know how to enjoy being a grandpa in the beginning when Jason was just an infant. However as time went by, Jason started to smile, and then later on he started recognizing me, which would always make my day.

Our second grandchild, Sean Sungju Lee, was born on April 4, 2005 in the Chicago are. Sean has a birthmark on his forehead, in exactly the same area that my wife has one. Our third grandchild, Aidan Chunju Lee was born on August 26, 2007. Aidan also has birthmark on his right hand middle finger which I always joke about with him about whenever we get together.

As all three of them have grown and as I have played with them over the years, the joy of being a grandpa has been amazing. Whenever we visit Chicago, they are so happy to see us. One of my favorite memories was when Kum, Helen, and I took the boys out to play nine holes of real golf when they were young. I took a picture with Jason and Sean at the first tee box holding our drivers, and I still keep that photo on the homepage of our computer. We repeated the outing a few years later at the same golf course in Naperville and took the same picture; my wife and I look about the same but the kids have changed a lot in just a few years!

Aidan was a very reserved boy around me at first. I had a hard time getting acquainted with him until our trip to my nephew Johnny's wedding in Akron, Ohio in 2009. Aidan was two years old and brought one of his toys to me that made sounds or music when we pushed a button. So he and I played with that toy quite a bit together. He brought that same toy to me the next day to play with again. From then on we became really good friends! I think his chin looks like mine. In Korean it is called "가지볼처럼

축처졌다" I think and Aidan look very similar (although my daughter disagrees and says that Sean is most like me!)

My son and his wife Esther had their first child, and our first granddaughter, Katie (Kaitlyn Hannah) Lee on May 20, 2008. Her Korean name is Joohee. Katie also has a younger brother CJ (Christian John) Lee who was born on September 28, 2010. John is my Catholic name, and CJ's middle name was named after me! CJ's Korean name is Heeseung. Having only one granddaughter and four grandsons gives me a special feeling with Katie, and I have noticed that she makes many sacrifices for her brother CJ. Usually the youngest child gets spoiled just like I was spoiled. My older brother always sacrificed for me and avoided any confrontation with me even though he was physically stronger than me and more athletic. CJ reminds me of when I was his age and Katie reminds me of my older brother. I hope CJ learns how to appreciate everything his sister does for him, and that one day he will sacrifice for her as well!

2007: Jason, Sean, and Aidan right after Aidan's birth.
(r) June 2011: The Lee Family portrait.

My own children never knew their grandparents very well. So it's wonderful to be more a part of my own grandchildren's lives. I never knew that being a grandfather could be such a joyful experience! It has helped to balance out the pain and suffering from my youth and even with all the typical ups and downs that I had with my own kids. There is a Korean proverb that says "love skips a generation" to describe the experience of being a grandparent. It is very easy to love our grandkids and I always looking forward to seeing them, particularly for our family reunion every Thanksgiving!!

CONCLUSION: A UNIQUE LIFE

In summary, I feel like I have had a very turbulent life. The start to my life was certainly unusual given all the geopolitical events that preceded and then ultimately contributed to the Korean War. I then lived as a person in exile throughout my life in the U.S. Very few people from North Korea not only lost their mother at thirteen years of age, but then came to America, became a U.S. federal government employee, and then spent thirty years working near the White House. Whenever I went to work at my office, I always wondered, "How in the world, did I, a Pyongyang-born Korean, come to this country, became a U.S. citizen, get a job at the federal government, and work near the White House, the most powerful house in the world?"

And how many other people walked seventeen days from Pyongyang to Seoul, lost his mother because of the Korean War, located his mother thirty-nine years later (!), went to Pyongyang to see her for the first time since 1950, and arrived only to learn that she had passed away three months prior?

My early turbulent life did not lead me to expect the good life that I had after meeting Kum Choi. Marrying her was really the turning point of my life in a positive way. My wife is amazing and such a selfless, considerate, and caring woman! I really don't know how I have been so fortunate to receive such a gift, but my life has been blessed by having her as my wife. I am so grateful to God for this irreplaceable and most valuable gift in my life.

Some of the Key Turning Points of My Life:

- During the Korean War I left Pyongyang on December 4, 1950, left my mom behind and became a refugee.
- I entered Keisung High School, a missionary school where my Christian faith began in 1953.
- I failed to gain admittance to the Seoul National University in 1957, which led to my coming to America.
- I came to the U.S. to study abroad in 1963.
- I married my wife in Seattle on April 27, 1968.

- I got my first full-time job teaching at EWSC in 1968.
- Our first child, Helen was born in Spokane, Washington, on May 12, 1969.
- I finished my Ph.D. at WSU in 1974.
- Our second child, Brian, was born in Clarkston, Washington, on September 26, 1974.
- I got a job at the ERS/USDA and we moved to Washington D.C. in 1975.
- My wife starts her first small business, a lobby shop, in 1976, and it is there that she later meets Sam Rose.
- Sam Rose gave my wife the lease to operate the Capitol Cafe in his Union Center Plaza building and then later Station Cafe at Union Center Plaza 2 where the CNN studio in D.C. is still stationed.
- We retired and moved to California in 2004.

Most of these turning points were beyond my control. I believe God was the one who guided my life during all my years, and He continues to do so. I hope my children and grandchildren understand this as they get older and think about their own lives.

A Final Poem to End

During my retirement, my daughter Helen sent me numerous books to read including: (1) *Golf and the Spirit, Lessons for the Journey*, by Scott Peck, (2) *The Purpose-Driven Life*, by Rick Warren, (3) *Why I Like Being a* Catholic, by Michael Leach, (4) *Quiet Strength* by Coach Tony Dungy, (5) *Why I Like Being a Catholic*, by Garry Wills, and (6) *Growing Healthy Asian-American Churches*, edited by my daughter, Peter Cha, and Steve Kang.

In his book, *Golf and the Spirit, Lessons for the Journey*, Peck talked about his golf widow—his wife, Lily, a Chinese woman—whose situation was very similar to my wife's. As a fitting way to end my memoir, I'd like to quote him here, to express what I think of my wife:

I thank You for my friends
And, most specially,
For my best friend.
Thirty-seven years ago (*mine would be nearly 50 years ago!*),
When Lily (*Teresa*) and I were wed,
I did not know who she was.
Nor she me.
Nor much about ourselves.
Nor anything about marriage at all.
The learning was often to be painful,
Although without it
There would have been nothing.
Somehow we made it through,
And it would be wrong not to give ourselves
Any credit. But tell me this:
Utterly innocent back then,
How did I know
In my blind ignorance
That Lily (*Teresa*) —more different
Than I could imagine—
Was right for me?
I cannot explain it
Unless You were invisibly at my side,
Guiding me while I, like Jacob,
Was unaware. And I,
Like Jacob, must also now exclaim:
"Surely God was in this place, and I,
 I did not know it"

As the author suggested, at times, Teresa and I were unsure we
would or should complete this journey of love and living together.
I know that, by God's grace, our marriage has become a thing of
mystical love. It is love, but it is even more joyful than romantic
love, and at such moments of awareness, my heart is filled nigh
unto bursting.

This is why, as I reflect on my 80 years, I can still say despite all the
ups and downs of my life, that I am filled with nothing but joy. My
hope and prayer is that my children and grandchildren and
grandchildren's children and beyond would be able to look back on

their lives and say the same thing. I thank God for each and every day of my life, through all the hardships and struggles, because I know that I am a blessed man!

To God be the glory. Amen!

APPENDIX 1:
MY WORLDWIDE TRAVELS

Throughout my life I was blessed to travel around the world. Traveling was fun and I feel strongly that you learn so much from traveling to different parts of the world. I hope that our grandchildren are like us and love to travel when they grow up!

Pyongyang, Diamond Mountain, and Beijing (1989 and 1991)

The highlights of my travel were two visits to Pyongyang, the first time alone and the second time with my wife. On both visits we went through Beijing. During my first trip, I visited the Great Wall. On the second trip, my wife and I visited the Ming Dynasty's underground palace right in Tiananmen Square and their secret summer palace.

On our second trip to Pyongyang we also visited Mt. Kumkang (the Diamond Mountain). We hiked all the way to Man-Mul-Sang on a perfect, sunny day to see all the different faces of Diamond Mountain. Usually because the mountain is so high, clouds cover the diamond faces most of the time, but we were lucky that day. The tour guide told us that this kind of weather usually didn't even happen once a year!

Cairo, Egypt and Suez Canal (August 1980)

I traveled to Cairo, Egypt for a U.S. AID project. U.S. AID charged our agency to recruit and train agricultural officials from Egypt. During this time, I was assigned to the OICD (Office of International Cooperation and Development) in the USDA for about three years. My job at the OICD was recruiting and programming training for government officials in developing countries. I also taught them economic analysis and research methodology. Of course it was U.S.-funded, as part of the U.S. Foreign Assistance Bill passed by Congress.

In Cairo, other than going to the University of Cairo to interview, I ate at the U.S. embassy restaurant almost every evening. It was a few blocks from my residence in Cairo and was a nice place overlooking the Nile River.

Naturally, I couldn't pass up visiting the Sphinx and the pyramids. During my visit to the pyramids, they allowed us to climb all the way up to the top and inside. A king's tomb there had a small door open in order to let in some sun all the time. I don't know if tourists can still climb up to the top and inside of the pyramids, but it was an unforgettable memory for me! I also went to the museum where King Tut was securely kept and displayed.

One evening our local U.S. AID staff, an Egyptian, invited me to have dinner with him and a few other university staff at a restaurant near the pyramids. I didn't know it then but know now that Muslims don't drink. When the waitress asked what I'd like to drink I said a glass of wine. The others drank some kind of tea. The waitress told me that they only served bottles of wine, not glasses. I ended up drinking the whole bottle by myself. I apologized to the host because it cost them a lot for the bottle.

During my stay in Cairo, I sometimes had an afternoon off due to scheduling. One time, my U.S. AID counterpart in the embassy told me that I should go to the Kalahari district to buy some souvenirs and that she could send them to the U.S. through the APO. A U.S. AID driver took me there. He said that the district was 6,000 years old. It was jammed with small areas to walk. I spent about two hours touring the district and bought two handmade flower vases and one Cleopatra plate. We still have both of them.

Another time, when I had an afternoon off, the driver took me to the City of Suez. It was a very crowded old city. To get there we had to drive through the Sinai desert where the Egyptian army was stationed, just in case of a fight with Israel. From Suez City, I saw the Red Sea, a very clean sea, as a big ship was crossing the canal. Then we drove on a new highway which was still under construction, but I was able to go since I was a U.S. government official. It was funded by U.S. AID and the highway went under the canal and came out on the other side of the Sinai desert.

Islamabad, Pakistan (January 1982)

In 1982, I traveled to Islamabad, Pakistan for a U.S. AID project. Our team had four members: the administrator, an agronomist from University of Vermont, myself, the economist, and a budget analyst from AID. We spent one week figuring out the potential income that could be generated from oilseed production. Sunflower seeds were very plentiful in Pakistan and U.S AID was trying to support a production increase to export the oilseed for economic development. From Islamabad we flew to Lahore which is located on the eastern part of Pakistan, not too far from Kashmir, where we witnessed the conflict between Pakistan and India.

What I remember about this one-week trip was that there was nothing to do after work. The Holiday Inn where we stayed had almost all-day Islamic prayer and no entertainment. Therefore, we ended up in the embassy compound after work, which meant lots of drinks at the bar. I think many embassy workers throughout the world have this kind of problem: nothing else to do after office hours.

I flew from New York through London to get to Islamabad. My partner from U.S. AID in D.C. traveled quite a bit and was a frequent flyer. So when we arrived at the TWA counter, he somehow negotiated for us both to get on first class! Government tickets are usually economy class. So we flew to London in first class. The next day, my partner left London for Islamabad via British Airways. I decided to stay one more day to go sightseeing in

London. My partner suggested that I fly with him since the next day's flight to Islamabad was on Pakistan International Airlines and being an experienced flyer, he knew the danger of flying a second class airline like PIA.

However, I decided to stay a day. After sightseeing, I got on board Pakistan International Airlines. PIA stopped in Copenhagen to board additional passengers. It was a very cloudy day with fog. And when we were about to depart, the airport decided to close for the day. Most airlines took their passengers to nearby hotels. PIA, however, decided to take off to avoid the cost of putting us up in a hotel for a day. The pilot stayed on the runway for about an hour. I was scared and others were too. We could see only a few feet outside the window. Finally, the captain announced he was taking off and suggested that we tighten our seat belts. When I told this story to my partner in Islamabad, he warned me to "never fly second class carriers" anymore in the future. You just couldn't trust them.

My partner's advice was useful when I departed from Islamabad to Karachi, and then to New Delhi, en route to Seoul. My trip had started by crossing the Atlantic Ocean and I would return home crossing the Pacific Ocean. I circled the globe and realized "it's a small world" after all!

Rome, Paris, Ankara, Turkey, Abidjan, Ivory Coast, Seoul, Korea and Tokyo, Japan (August 1983)

In 1983, I went to Turkey, the Ivory Coast, and Korea to recruit government officials for what we called "AID-Graduated" countries. Senator Corcoran from Mississippi slipped $1 million— they call doing this "pork belly"—into the 1982 fiscal budget to help leaders from "AID-Graduated" countries receive training in the U.S. The hope was that when they return home and earn higher positions in their governments, they will buy more U.S. farm products. I was in charge of recruiting trainees from four countries: Ivory Coast, Turkey, South Korea, and Columbia. So my trip overseas was to interview candidates.

I left DC for Rome, en route to Abidjan, Ivory Coast. In Rome I met with the Korean Agricultural Attaché. In Rome, there were a few international organizations under the U.N. charter and the one mostly involved with food was FAO (U.N Food and Agricultural Organization). Because of this, Korea had an Agricultural Attaché in Rome. Since I was also going to Korea on this recruiting trip, the Korean Agricultural Attaché in DC made a call for him to greet me at the airport. The attaché booked me in a hotel just a block away from the Korean Embassy. In the evening he arranged a dinner with Irene Fields, who was the FAO trainer for developing countries with whom I'd had many wire exchanges regarding training government officials from developing countries. We talked about our new Corcoran program over dinner.

The next day I had time to go sightseeing around Rome and then I left for Paris. The agricultural attaché made an arrangement for a Korean student to meet me at the airport and escort me for a couple days. He took me to the Louvre museum and many others including Versailles Palace. Then I left Paris for Abidjan. Ivory Coast had been a French colony and so they spoke French. Furthermore, there were frequent flights to Abidjan from Paris. It was a long flight, about twelve hours. The African continent is huge, which I didn't fully understand before. When I arrived in Abidjan, there was an expediter from the U.S. embassy who took me to the Hilton. The next day, I went to the embassy and met with the U.S. Agricultural Attaché in Ivory Coast and we conducted our recruiting interviews. The main problem with many of the candidates was that they didn't speak English well. They all spoke fluent French however. My favorite memory of Abidjan was that the Attaché invited me for dinner at his house, which was not only huge but also close to a jungle. It was a very beautiful house and he also took me into the jungle to see how African tribes live.

From Abidjan, Ivory Coast, I few to Rome, then on to Athens. I switched planes in Athens to Istanbul and finally to Ankara. When I arrived at the U.S. Embassy in Ankara next day after resting at a hotel upon arrival, I met a friend who was a Turkey student when I was at Vanderbilt. He was working in U.S. Embassy there and one day invited me to his house one for dinner. We had delicious shish-kebabs at his house. And, he and his family took me to an opera where the Russian Opera was performing. Coming from the U.S., and also having had experience with Russians in Pyongyang, I felt very emotional seeing this. It reminded me of my mother.

The next day, I met the U.S. Agricultural Attaché and we went to the Ministry of Agriculture to meet with the Deputy Minister. We discussed how we should proceed with this Corcoran program and their Minister's recommendation was that I should go to Adana to recruit. Adana was located about two hours south of Turkey, by plane and was located in a farming area of Turkey.

The city of Adana is very strategic for the U.S. There was a U.S. Air Force base which is not too far away from Syria, Iran and all the other Middle Eastern countries. Because of that, the U.S. had a counselor's office in Adana. This city is also an agricultural region with rich soil. I met an American businessman at dinner in the Holiday Inn where I stayed. We sat together for dinner and talked about why I was there and why he was. He was a fortune digger. In southern Turkey, because the area was a path trod by biblical figures, there were ample Christian treasures underneath the land. This is because Turkey had several earthquakes and many historical assets had been buried. The man told me that he'd found many historically valuable relics.

I interviewed candidates at the University of Adana. The Dean of College of Agriculture was educated at the University of Massachusetts. He took me to dinner that night and the beer we drank was so good. I asked him how come they don't export this tasteful beer? The reason I asked was because South Korea was emerging as a newly developed country mainly from their export-oriented development policy and I thought Turkey should also do the same. The Dean didn't have any good answer to me.

The next day I met with the U.S. Consulate in Adana. He emphasized the strategic location of Adana for the U.S. and asked me to recruit as many students from there as possible. He also took me to the U.S. airbase close to the border with Syria and offered to buy me a local Turkish rug that he would ship back home for me through the Army Post Office. APO is free from overseas to any

APO point in the U.S. and I only needed to pay the domestic postage, which I did.

One afternoon the embassy driver took me to a place called St Paul's well which is in a courtyard that is believed to be the site of Paul's home. We also crossed a stone bridge which, the driver said, was over 1,000 years old. From there he took me Tarsus where I saw a small lake where Cleopatra had once landed.

From Adana, I flew back to Ankara, then to Istanbul, then to Paris and finally to Seoul, flying over the North Pole. As we passed over the North Pole the captain told us to take a look outside the window. All I remember was that it was covered with snow. From Paris I flew to Seoul, which back then was one of the longest flights in the world. We had to stop in Anchorage to refuel.

I did the same kind of recruiting at the Ministry of Agriculture in Seoul. Even though the government paid for my lodging, I stayed at my dad's home for a few days. When I finished interviewing and was ready to depart, the Director of International Programs at the Ministry said that there would be someone to meet me at the Tokyo airport when I made a stopover. He was the Korean Agricultural Attaché in Japan. From the airport, he took me to the New Tokyo Hotel, I checked in and he told me we'd go to "sushi school".

He started by taking me to a huge sushi school where the sushi maker had his students sit behind him and learn how to make sushi. From there he took me to a small restaurant where some poor college professors were sitting around a fire where the cook grilled all kinds of fish for them. Next, we went to a sushi house for mid-level business executives, a sit-down sushi house where waitresses served customers.

Finally he took me to Ginza where, he said, it usually cost about $1,000 for two to have a full sushi dinner. Yes, $1,000 at that time! During this period Japan was a strong economic power and the dollar was very weak in comparison. I met this Attaché a few more times in D.C. when he came to visit as a Korean rep to negotiate agricultural trade with the U.S. From Tokyo, I then flew to New York, and then to D.C., finishing my trip around-the-world.

Buenos Aires, Argentina, Paraguay, and Brazil (August 1988)

In 1988, I attended the International Agricultural Association Meetings which were held in a convention center but the annual banquet was held at the Argentine Stock Market floor. It was very impressive place to have banquet dinner together. Also this was a place where beef steak was very cheap. It cost me $5.00 for a huge steak and a glass of wine was also included. In comparison, one evening my wife and I went a Chinese restaurant for dinner and it was so expensive, costing us $25.00.

On this trip we visited Iguazu Falls. These falls were located in the triangle between Brazil, Paraguay and Argentina. With this visit, and our previous visit to the International Falls (Victoria Falls) in Zimbabwe, we had visited all three world famous falls, which also included Niagara. On the way home, we visited San Paulo, Brazil, where one of my former professors from Soongsil University, Han Kook Chin, lived. We also stopped by Rio de Janeiro and chartered a taxi for a day of sightseeing. It cost us only nine dollars for the whole day.

I wondered why countries with such vast resources, like Argentina and Brazil, are so poor. Both countries' inflation rates were 500% per year! When I returned to Washington, DC, I wrote a column in the Korea Times titled "The Rich country and the Poor Country: Why Are They Poor?" I argued that it was the people, particularly the leader(s) of the country, that made them poor with poor decision making.

Christ the Redeemer, Rio de Janeiro, Brazil

Vienna, Austria and Keszthely, Hungary (August, 1989)

In 1989 before going to Hungary, I went first to Vienna, Austria.
Even though my Pan Am flight landed in Budapest, Hungary first,
and then went on to Vienna, my official U.S. government itinerary
required me to go to Vienna first. The government had a contract
with Pan Am to land in Vienna, not in Budapest. So, I decided to
stay in Vienna a few days before going to Budapest. I met a
Japanese musician on the flight from New York to Vienna. She

said she was a violinist and a member of the Vienna quartet. She was returning to Vienna from New York where her boyfriend lived. I was lucky to meet her on the airplane because I didn't have a hotel reservation in Vienna. My plan was to take a bus from the airport and find a "bed and breakfast" house. I had information on this from a friend in my office but no reservation. Luckily, there was a bed and breakfast house was on her way home and so she gave me a ride. I stayed in this house for a couple of days. Europeans usually include continental breakfast in their room charge, so breakfast was easy, but I had to find a place to eat dinner. So, I ate lots of kimchi bowls for dinner which I'd brought with me.

The first day I walked around the city and saw the state opera house, the Danube River, the University of Vienna, and a famous museum. The second day I took a bus to Salzburg, the famous birthplace of Mozart. I visited his house and also the location of the last scene of the Sound of Music, where the Von Trapp family sang before they fled from the Nazis to freedom.

From Salzburg, I took a train to Munich, Germany, where I spent one day visiting the city square where all the tourists gathered for the noon bell ringing and puppet show. I also visited an English garden, many famous cathedrals and of course, the world famous beer hall. My favorite memory was the German sausage that I ate there. It was so tasty!

From Munich, I took a train to Venice. At the train station, I saw Germans drinking beer in the morning, just like coffee. On the way to Zurich the two engines pulled our train through the beautiful Alps, passed Innsbruck, Austria, to Zurich, Switzerland. This train trip was unforgettable.

However, the train broke down somewhere between Austria and Switzerland. Everybody got off the train. Lucky for me, there was a Japanese student from London who was traveling for the summer who spoke English. He said that we had to get off, walk a couple of blocks show our passports to enter Switzerland from Austria, and then take another train. So I followed him to another train. He got off in Zurich and I switched to another train towards Lugano, Switzerland.

I didn't have any reservations or anyone waiting for me in Lugano. Therefore, I decided to walk to the downtown area that was just a few blocks away from the train station. The downtown was by the shore of Lake Lugano and there was an area where many people were gathered. I wanted to ask them about a "bed and breakfast" place to stay. Fortunately, I met a couple there: the man was Italian and the woman was Swiss. Luckily they were very nice and offered to take me with them to Lake Lugano for sightseeing and then afterwards invited me to a spaghetti restaurant for dinner. It was very garlicky! They said both Italians and Swiss eat lots of garlic. Since Lugano was close to Italy, apparently their tastes and cuisine were very similar. The next day I headed to Venice and the Italian guy told me where I should stay outside of the city. I could then take the city bus to Venice because it was very expensive to stay in Venice.

But first, I took the train to Milan on my way to Venice. In Milan, I toured Michelangelo's museum where I saw many of his sculptures, the museum where they stored Da Vinci's The Last Supper, and the second largest cathedral in the world, after the Vatican. From Milan I took another train and continued on to Venice. However, as the guy in Lugano told me, I got off the train one stop before the Venice station. Since nobody was waiting for me, and it was getting dark, I spoke with a couple people who were waiting at the station for their relatives or friends.

One guy who was studying theology, and was waiting for his girlfriend, said that if I waited a few minutes for his girlfriend, he would take me to a cheap and nice bed and breakfast house nearby the station. He eventually took me to the place and even talked to the owner in Italian. (We'd spoken in English.) It was a very reasonable price and even included dinner as well as breakfast. The next morning I walked one block to the train station and took a city bus to Venice. I spent all day in Venice walking around the city. I didn't take the gondolas because they were very expensive. I remember seeing San Marco Cathedral and walking across the Rialto Bridge.

In the evening I took the bus back to where I was staying, had dinner and then took a midnight train, with a bed, to Vienna. I had to give my passport to the conductor because we had to cross two countries, Italy and Switzerland. The train suite that I reserved had four beds. When I opened the door there were three college girls already asleep. They asked me to hurry up and go to sleep. I was so tired from walking all day in Venice that I slept well. When I woke up, all three girls were gone. They must have gotten off someplace before Vienna. I stayed again at a bed and breakfast house in Vienna and the next day I took the train to Budapest.

Unlike most countries, there was no border check when we got to Hungary by train. But I later found out that the train stopped at the border on the way back to Vienna and had a long waiting line as they thoroughly checked everyone's passports. From Budapest, I went to the meeting by chartered bus. The city of Keszler was a resort town, famous for its hot springs. One thing I remember was that at the goodbye banquet, five Hungarian gypsy dancers danced while we were having wine and dinner.

During the conference I met a Japanese guy who worked in Vienna with the International Labor Organization, as part of a UN agency. He'd driven from Vienna to the conference center in Hungary. I got acquainted with him during the three-day conference so he offered me a ride back to Vienna. We also met a Vietnamese student at the meeting. He was studying economics at the University of Hungary. I asked what they teach in Communist Hungary in economics. He said it was mostly welfare economics. He invited the Japanese guy and me to stay at his apartment and he kindly cooked us a Vietnamese dish for dinner. The next day he took me sightseeing in Budapest. I asked him to exchange my one hundred dollar bill for Hungarian currency with which I was able to buy a whole set of Hungarian china and some more souvenirs. I saw how strong the U.S. dollar was at that time.

Osaka, Japan (August 1990)

My meeting in Osaka, Japan was the Third International Conference on Korean Studies. Osaka is where the many Koreans live in Japan. I can't say they were Korean-Japanese because even if they were born in Japan, the Japanese government doesn't recognize them as Japanese. So, they are Koreans forever, with no power to vote in Japan and no employment opportunities in Japanese government.

This meeting was important because it was a period of time when Korean scholars throughout the world, specializing in Korean studies, were discussing the unification of Korea. Scholars, mostly Korean, came to this meeting from South Korea, Europe, Russia, China, Africa, South America, the United States, and North Korea.

The conference was mostly funded by Koreans in Osaka. There are many Koreans in Osaka who are successful in business but they don't have any political voice because they can't vote. I should also note that Koreans in Osaka tend to lean more towards North Korea than South Korea. Therefore, the hosts had little trouble inviting North Korean scholars to the meeting.

The session where I presented my paper had an economics professor from Kim Il-Sung University. I spoke with him on a few occasions at the conference but what I recall from his presentation was that he argued that in North Korea they don't need economic profit so there's no need for the business sector to compete to make profit. He said that this was because they all live in a utopia where everybody is equal, affluent, and happy. I just couldn't believe that he said that, and I can only assume he didn't actually believe it!

Another memorable event was that we all sang together a traditional Korean folk song that both North and South Koreans sing called "Arirang": "We want to see unification." We hugged each other to say goodbye before departing to return to our countries around the globe, knowing we might never see each other again.

Seoul, Korea (August 1990 and August 1992)

We visited Seoul to attend the annual conference of the Korean-American Economic Association. After the conference, the host took us on a five-day tour to the industrial zone in the southwest, Pusan, and Bul-Kook-Sa, as well as some scenic areas of South Korea. My wife couldn't go with me because the kids were still in school.

Tokyo, Japan (August 1991)

My trip to Tokyo was in conjunction with the International Association of Agricultural Economists. I presented a paper on South Korean agricultural development titled "A Lesson Learned". After the conference my wife and I had gone to Beijing in order to fly to Yunnan for an international conference on Korean studies, but we couldn't make it to Yunnan because there were no airplane seats available. They said it would take five days to get there by train. So I took my wife to Pyongyang. After the conference, we went to Seoul to visit with our family and told them about our experience in North Korea.

Oxford, England (May 1992)

We traveled to Oxford, England where I presented a paper at the International Management Conference. Oxford has many colleges and Williams College has a campus there called the "Williams at Oxford" program. We saw some students dressed up for their dinner and we asked why. One of them told us that that evening was the night when they'd learn "dinner manners." We also spent one evening at the student's' pub where we drank beer with college students. Another great memory was that we had a conference banquet in the Oxford University library. The host explained all the history of the library and one thing that I remember is the British gentleman who sat with us at the dinner table taught us wine drinking customs: how to taste, how to hold the glass, and what kind of wine should be in a small glass versus a tall glass.

Costa Del Sol, Spain (1994)

We went to Spain with Dr. Tai Young & Mrs. Hyesook Yum from San Francisco. During this trip, we visited the stadium where bullfighting originated. Every fifteen minutes a big bull was killed by bullfighters and the audience loved to see the blood on the courtyard. It was terrible to watch. We also visited the castle and backyard where the composer Bizet wrote the opera Carmen. One day we crossed the straits of Gibraltar to Tangier, Morocco. We also visited the towns of Malaga and Granada.

Paris, Brussels, Amsterdam, Groningen, Netherlands, Bonn, Cologne, Frankfurt, Germany, Lucent, Zurich, Geneva, Switzerland (August 1995)

Our trip to Groningen, Netherlands, was a very memorable one. Brian came along with us, and without him we wouldn't have enjoyed it as much! We arrived in Paris and rented a car. The agent gave us a brand new Mercedes Benz that we drove all the way to Switzerland and back. After staying a few hours in Paris, we drove it to Brussels, Belgium, and stayed one night. Europeans drink lots of beer and wine and the night we arrived in Brussels there was a beer and wine festival at the famous square in downtown Brussels, just a couple blocks away from our hotel. We tasted a few different beers on the square and went to a restaurant recommended by the hotel clerk.

On the next day we visited the city of Amsterdam. Since we had a car, we drove to a suburb and stayed in a hotel. At night we went to the square. Europeans, and tourists as well, stayed all night eating, drinking and singing on this famous downtown square, just like we'd seen in Brussels. On the third day, we drove to the north side of the Netherlands. The western part of the Netherlands is below sea level and we saw the dams blocking the ocean and cultivated farm land.

We traveled to Groningen, which is what they call this city at the "top of the Netherlands." Later on our trip to Switzerland we saw a sign marking the "top of Europe" at Mount Jungfraujoch indicating the tallest mountain in Europe. We stayed in Groningen for four days. The next to last day, the local committee of the conference took us on a tour and hosted a final banquet for us which was impressive.

We then drove to Bonn and Cologne, Germany. We had lunch there and drove along the Rhine River looking at the large cattles.

We drove to Frankfurt, had dinner there at the train station circle at Korea House. We couldn't find a hotel there, and they were so very expensive, so we drove further south past Hamburg and stayed one night along the Rhine River. The next day we drove to Strasbourg, France, gassed up and headed to Switzerland. Our first stop was at city of Lucent. We had lunch, took a cable car to the top of a mountain, walked to the bus, and drove back to Lucent. We settled in for the night at Zurich. The next day we went to an outdoor city fair where we ate roast suckling pig. Oh, it was so tasty! The next day, we drove to the highest Mountain in Switzerland, Jungfraujoch. We stayed overnight there.

The next morning we took the train to the top of the mountain. Although it was July, there was tons of snow on top of the mountain. In the Netherlands we'd seen how they dammed the ocean water to preserve farms and make a living out of it. And we saw in Switzerland, a mountainous country, how they made a living from the mountains. The next morning we drove south, past Evian, France, and stayed in Geneva. The next morning we drove to south France, visited a famous winery where we bought a five-gallon jar of local wine that we drank and then took home what was leftover. We continued to Versailles Palace, staying overnight nearby. The next day we drove back to Paris and then returned home.

I remember most of this trip because we didn't have much of it pre-planned other than the conference in Groningen. Therefore, we had to make a plan every day, looking for a hotel then deciding where to go and what to do. I highly recommend traveling this way!

Dominican Republic (1996), the Caribbean, Bermuda and Hawaii Golf Trips

In 1996, Brian came with us on a trip to the Dominican Republic where we played the Teeth of the Dog, a course once ranked in the top 20 in the world.

In the Caribbean, we have been to the Bahamas, Puerto Rico, Barbados, St Lucia, St. Croix, St. Thomas, the Virgin Islands, and the Dominican Republic, twice. My favorite golf course was Mahogany Run in St. Thomas. For our first Bahamas trip we took our children along. They were young and I think Brian was in still in elementary school. Helen didn't play golf but Brian did.

We have been to Bermuda where we played both the Mid Ocean Club and Port Royal Golf Course. We have also played golf in Hawaii in Maui, Kauai, the Big Island, and more.

New Brunswick, Nova Scotia, Prince Edwards Island, Nova Scotia (August 1996)

We had an international conference in the city of Fredericton in the Province of New Brunswick, Nova Scotia. For this conference we flew to Portland, Maine, rented a car, and crossed into Halifax, Nova Scotia, by ferry. We took our old friends from Maryland, Mr. and Mrs. Sung Young Lee, with us for this trip since they enjoyed traveling. We drove to the far eastern part of Nova Scotia to Grace Bay, Sydney, and then to North Sydney on Canada's 104 highway. We jumped onto another ferry at Pictou to Prince Edward's Island. We drove through the far northeastern coast of the island and played golf at Green Gables Country Club on Prince Edward's Island.

At the top of the island we rented a house. We then bought fish from the harbor market, which we ate fresh and also cooked as fish soup. Delicious! It was a very memorable stay. The next day, we took the ferry again and crossed from the Province of New Brunswick to Fredericton, the city where the conference was held. We played another round of golf at the best golf course in the city. We then drove to the Canada-U.S. border, a small town, and ferried back to the U.S. to Portland, Maine. We bought some fresh lobsters and shipped them to home on our flight.

U.S. Open - Congressional Country Club, Potomac, MD (1997)

This was Ernie Els' 2nd major championship.

Rose Bowl - Washington State vs. University of Michigan (January 1, 1998)

This was supposed to be my first trip to the Rose Bowl… but my father passed away before our trip to Los Angeles so I went to Korea instead. Luckily, my wife, my kids, my son-in-law and one of their friends went in my place. The Cougs lost 21-16 in an exciting game that came down to the last play of the game.

Scandinavian countries (Denmark, Sweden, Norway, Finland) and St. Petersburg, Russia (2000)

We took a trip with friends to Scandinavia. We started our trip traveling from Amsterdam, Holland, to Copenhagen, Denmark. The first day in Copenhagen we went to a famous park where we also had dinner on a very crowded small lakeside. The next day we crossed a bridge to go from the bigger island of Denmark to Vejle and Aarhus. We visited a few big old castles where kings and queens lived. From there we crossed a bay via a small ferry to go to Varberg, Sweden and then to Gothenburg, Sweden, and then to Oslo, Norway. In Oslo, we visited Norway's famous Viking ship and also its city hall, which is famous for the annual Nobel Peace Prize Awards. From Oslo, we went to Stockholm, Sweden. We visited the old town in Stockholm and the city hall.

From Stockholm we crossed another bay to get to Turku, Finland. Turku was the capital city of Finland years ago but they later switched to Helsinki, which we visited next. Then we crossed the border into Russia to go to St. Petersburg. We were told by the tour guide that it is extremely difficult to please the Russian border customs agents and that we needed to be very careful. We saw so many cars and particularly commercial trucks lined up to get permission to pass through the borderline. We were also told that most of the land between Finland and Russia had been part of Finland but they'd lost it to Russia.

My most memorable moment was in St. Petersburg. We rode a chartered boat along the river for about two hours while five Russian men and women entertained us with a Russian folk dance. It didn't cost much. We also visited summer and winter (hermitage) palaces of Peter the Great, saw a famous cathedral and watched a Russian folk dance at a theater.

This trip brought back my memories of the Russians in Pyongyang when they came to Korea after defeating Japan. Back then Russians were like kings and we, the Koreans, envied their proud and powerful country.

Copenhagen, Denmark

Berlin, Munich, Germany, Lugano, Switzerland, and Florence, Italy (August 2000)

I had very emotional feelings while visiting Berlin, which is now united! When I saw the Berlin Wall, I naturally wondered about the idea of a unified Korea, where all the separated families would be able to unite with their loved ones again!

We stayed in West Berlin, and took the subway to East Berlin where we had our conference. We saw the vast differences between East and West Berlin during our stay.

After the Berlin conference, my wife and I took a train trip to Rome by Eurorail. Our first stop was Munich, Germany. This was my second time visiting Munich. We visited the world-famous beer house in Munich, on the city square where thousands gather for the bell-ringing and puppet shows during the noon hour. There were many old cathedrals, both Catholic as well as Lutheran churches. When I booked the train trip, I was thinking about showing my wife the beautiful Alps.

Years ago I took a trip to Venice from Vienna in the summer and two engines pulled our train across the Alps. I'd seen the beautiful snow-covered Alps and so I thought our train from Munich to Lugano, Switzerland, would be the same route. However, I discovered that our trip from Munich to Zurich had a different route, alongside the mountain valley and not through the Alps. I was so disappointed for my wife who was expecting to see the Alps!

We changed trains at Zurich and went to Lugano, Switzerland, where we stayed at the same hotel I stayed years ago, near the beautiful lake Lugano. We had dinner at the lakeside restaurant as many tourists do and headed to Florence, Italy, the next day. We didn't have enough time to stop in Milan so we passed without stopping. In Florence we saw many of Michelangelo's sculptures. We had lunch at the city center square where Michelangelo's sculpture of Columbia was located. We left Florence after four hours and headed to Venice. We stayed two days visiting the famous St. Marco's church, as well as others, and then headed to Macerata, Italy, where I had another conference.

Venice, Macerata and Rome, Italy (August 2000)

This conference was connected to our trip to Berlin. It wasn't a big city but it was a historical city located in the central eastern part of Italy. From Venice, we had to change trains three times to get there but, amazingly, the train connections were on time and so we didn't miss any. We spent two nights and three days in Macerata. The local host of the conference took us sightseeing and we had a banquet dinner at one of the oldest castles there. While in Macerata, we took a taxi—four hours each way!—right after I presented a paper to the city of Assisi, a famous historical site for Catholics.

One difference between Catholic faith and Protestant faith is that you not only believe Jesus Christ is your savior but you also practice your belief. Believing alone doesn't save you but the practice of your belief saves you too. Therefore, there was a famous Catholic father in Assisi whose name was Father Francis. Later he became a Saint but Father Francis wanted to live like Jesus Christ. My mother-in-law was a member of a St. Francis group in Los Angeles where she spent almost all Saturdays helping poor and sick people in the area. The city of Assisi had a severe earthquake several years ago and many buildings were damaged, but the St. Francesco church structure was still there and we were able to visit it.

We stayed for three days and after the conference we took a train to Rome. It was my wife's first visit and my fourth. Being a Catholic, she was so excited to visit the Vatican. From there we headed home.

2000 and 2007: The Vatican

Auckland, New Zealand and Sydney, Australia (January 2001 and February 2007)

I visited Auckland, New Zealand, in 2001 and 2007. After attending the International Conference on Livestock Marketing, I was mainly interested in visiting my older brother who had just emigrated from Korea to be with his children in Auckland. My wife and I spent a week in his house and we also visited Sydney where one of my wife's closest friends lived. Sydney was very impressive and cosmopolitan.

We also made another trip to Sydney and Auckland in February 2007. My brother was very ill with kidney failure and complications from diabetes. So this was the my last trip to be able to see him.

2007: My brother, Chungkook Lee, and his wife.

2001: The Sydney Opera House.

Alaska: By Air, Cruise, Train, and Bus (2002)

Five couples went to Alaska together. The trip was a combination of sea, land, and air travel. We flew to Vancouver, BC, and our cruise started from there on a Dawn Princess ship to Anchorage. Ours was a first class cabin on the top floor of the ship with easterly-facing windows so that we were able to see day and night scenes of the coasts of Vancouver and all the Inside Passages to Anchorage. We stopped at Ketchikan, where we had a half-day stopover. There were ancient totem poles from Native American villages and on Eagles Bay there were eagles in treetops that scanned the bay to catch incoming salmon. The next stop was Juneau where some of us went salmon-fishing on a chartered boat and others went to the national park to hike and watch wild animals. The next stop was at Skagway for a whole day stopover. Rather than sightseeing in the area, we decided to go on a golf trip to Whitehorse, Yukon, Canada. The tour guide drove a van from Skagway up a mountain, crossing the border, and on to the city of Whitehorse. On our return we stopped by a beautiful canyon where we made a campfire in a small park overlooking the beautiful canyon and ate salmon a few of us caught in Juneau. It was a memorable golf trip to the Yukon Territory. The next day we passed the Glacier National Park where we stopped for a photo session. We were told that this place usually got either rain or snow and that most of the time it was too foggy to see the glaciers. However, when we arrived it was a beautiful day, although very cold outside of our cabin. We still braved going out on the deck to take many pictures.

We passed Kenai Fjord Bay and College Fjord Bay where a few Fjords were named after Ivy League Colleges and one was named after Williams College! I heard that many college professors came to this bay to study glacier movements and thereafter they named it "College Fjords." When we arrived in Anchorage, the sun was out eighteen hours a day our and hotel rooms had thick screens to cover the windows from the sun so we could sleep. We stayed one day in Anchorage and then flew to Prudhoe Bay and stayed at a camp where most of the people worked in the oilfields. We were able to observe two grizzlies the next morning when we woke up. They were searching for food in the trash dumpster.

Our favorite memory of this trip was driving 800 miles across Alaska on a Princess Bus along the Alaskan pipeline. Throughout the Alaskan tundra, we saw many caribou running as we drove the unpaved highways to Coldfoot Alaska. Coldfoot had a sign announcing "population zero." There was an old cottage for pipeline builders where we stayed overnight but most people who worked in Coldfoot lived in another small town about ten miles away. We arrived in Fairbanks and visited the gold mine. The next day we took the famous lrass-roof train to Denali National Park. This is a famous train that most tourists look forward to riding. At the National Park, my wife and I went rafting on the Denali River. From the park, we took another train to Anchorage where we departed for Chicago next day.

Rose Bowl - Washington State vs. Oklahoma Sooners (January 1, 2003)

My first trip to the Rose Bowl, having missed the game my family attended in 1998 due to the passing of my father. The Cougs lost 34-14.

South Africa, Zambia, Zimbabwe, International Falls, South African Safari (August 2003)

In Durban, South Africa, we attended the International Conference of Agricultural Economists. I knew that this trip would probably be my last overseas trip as an ERS/USDA employee, since I was planning to retire the following year.

The first evening we took a taxi to a portside restaurant for seafood. The driver told us, as we drove through downtown Durban streets, not to walk on the streets because many were unsafe. We also visited Cape Town.

We also went to Liverpool, Zambia, to see the International Falls (Victoria Falls) from the Zambian side. The next day, we went to Zimbabwe to see the better side of the falls. On the third day we played safari golf alongside monkeys, birds, and other various animals! There was a beautiful white colored hotel where we were told that Queen Victoria of England had vacationed there during the summer time.

We also went to Ulusaba, a private game reserve, adjacent to Kruger National Park, the world's largest game park. The safari was very exciting. We drank scotch in the wild park in the middle of night after finishing the safari while one guard held a rifle to protect us. We also drank coffee in the quiet morning in the middle of jungle while the morning sun was rising. The jungle house where we stayed had chimpanzees on the roof in the morning waking us up. Outside of the room we could see many elephants walking in the valley.

2003: Table Mountain, Cape Town, South Africa.

Greece-Turkey (2005)

A friend of mine in Ottawa, Uhm In Ho, invited us on a trip to Greece and Turkey with his alumni group from Seoul High School. On October 19, 2005, our trip started in Athens with sightseeing. Then we went to Delphi. During this Delphi trip we learned that the city of Colossae was close by. The tour guide told us that during the first century the city was corrupt and that prostitution and drunkenness were prevalent. The apostle Paul came to Colossae to address this by preaching the gospel.

On the third day, we took a ferry to an island called Mykonos, a resort city. Then we went to Rhodes. From the Island of Rhodes we ferried to the Island of Patmos where we went to see the cave where St. John wrote Revelation. We proceeded to Kusadasi, in Turkey, and to the historically famous city of Ephesus. There was only one column left of the original church of Ephesus and I saw the site of St. John's death. This is the church where they called Mary as the "Mother of God" and Catholic started to observe Mary's "Immaculate conception" and "without the original sin".

When Jesus died, he asked John to take care of his mother and John did. We visited the place where Mary lived and we participated in the open mass there. The city of Ephesus and its churches were all buried underground by earthquakes.

The next day, we visited Pamukkale, Laodicea, Sardis and Pergamon. Before we rode the ferry to Istanbul, we visited the city of Troy. After crossing the straits, we arrived in Istanbul and visited Sophia, Byzantine and Ottoman Relics, On the last day we visited Dolmabahce Palace and Bosphorus. We also could see the Black Sea which was not too far away. Turkey is located strategically: all the ships going to Eastern Europe have to go through the straits between European Istanbul and Asian Istanbul.

Ireland (2006)

It was sad to note that Ireland, one island, has two countries: Northern Ireland, part of Great Britain and the Republic of Ireland in the south. Northern Island's original people are mostly Catholic and the people who moved in from England are Protestants. Northern Islanders have a group of extremists who want to unite with the Republic of Ireland and want independence from Great Britain.

My wife, Brian, his childhood friend Chris Reynolds, and I arrived in Belfast and departed from Dublin. We played golf at some of the best courses in the world, namely Royal County Down, Royal Portrush, Portstewart, Portmarnock.

2006: 9th Fairway at Royal County Down, Ireland.

U.S. Open - Torrey Pines, CA (2008)

This was where Tiger Woods won his 14th major championship. He played with a broken leg, stress fractures and a torn ACL in his left knee, having had arthroscopic surgery just two months prior that had not healed.

The Masters - Augusta, GA (2009)

Not only did we have front row seats on Saturday on the 12th hole, the par 3 in Amen's Corner, but on Sunday we sat in the bleachers by the 15th green where we were able to see the exciting approach shots into the par 5 and also the tee shots on the beautiful par 3 16th hole. Angel Cabrera from Argentina defeated Kenny Perry on the second playoff hole for the victory and his second major championship.

On this trip, our granddaughter Katie also took her first steps at the age of 11 months!

Cacapon Resort State Park - Berkeley Springs, WV (October 2009)

My sister-in-law, Sook Kim, her husband, Young Kim, and my wife.

U.S. Open - Congressional Country Club, Potomac, MD (2011)

This was Rory McIlroy's first major championship. Twelve of our family members (me, my wife, my son, his wife, my granddaughter Katie, my daughter, her husband, my two grandsons Jason and Sean, my nephews Ellis and Johnny and Johnny's wife) sat in the front row off the 18th green on Sunday and cheered on Rory's victory.

Photo credit: Rod Lamkey, Jr.

Cypress Point and Pebble Beach - Monterey, CA (2012)

We departed Van Nuy Airport in LA on a private plane to
Monterey Bay Airport and spent 3 glorious days playing some of
the most spectacular (and private/exclusive) golf courses in the
U.S.

16th Tee and 17th Tee at Cypress Point

Fiji, Brisbane, Sydney (2012)

Train Riding Trip to France (September 2014)

Paris-Lyon-Nice-Monaco-Cannes-Marseille-Toulouse-Bordeaux-Lourdes-Paris

Lourdes, France   Nice, France

Williams Alumni Golf Tournament - Williamstown, MA (July 2017)

Brian and I finished in first place in the 5th flight, and my wife, Katie, and CJ played together in the nine-hole scramble!

Taconic Golf Club, Williamstown, MA

London to North Cape, Norwegian Fjords (August 2017)

This trip was our 50th wedding anniversary and my 80th birthday celebration. We took a Princess Cruise sailing from Southampton, England to North Cape, Norway. It was one of the most memorable trip in our lives.

APPENDIX 2
MY CURRICULUM VITAE

Education

Ph.D. 1974 (Agr. Economics)
Washington State University
Pullman, Washington

M.A. 1966 (Economics)
Vanderbilt University
Nashville, Tennessee

B.A. 1961 (Economics)
Soongsil University
(Union Christian College), Seoul, Korea

Research Experiences:
Senior Economist, 1998-2004
Economic Research Service
U.S. Department of Agriculture, Washington, D.C.

Agricultural Economist, 1984-1998
Economic Research Service, 1975-1981
U.S. Department of Agriculture, Washington, D.C.

Research Associate, 1972-1974
Washington State University, Pullman, WA

Teaching Experiences:

Adjunct Professor, Fall, 2004-2005
Soka University, Aliso Viejo, CA 92656

Adjunct Professor, 2003-2004
University of Maryland
University College, College Park, MD

"   , 1993-1995
Averett College Northern Virginia Program

"   , 1986-1995
USDA Graduate School, Washington, D.C.

"   , 1983-1985
Ben Franklin University, Washington, D.C.

"   , 1976-1982
Southeastern University, Washington, D.C.

Assistant Professor, 1968-1971
Eastern Washington University, Cheney, WA

Instructor, 1967-1968
St. Martin's College, Olympia, WA

Administrative Experience:

International Training Administrator, Office of International
Cooperation and Development, U.S. Department of Agriculture,
1980-1984

Memberships:

- American Agricultural Economics Association, 1974-2005
- Western Agricultural Economics Association, 1976-2005
- Association of Asian Studies, 1983-2003
- Korean Economic Society, 1975-2005
- International Association of Agricultural Economists, 1987-2005
- Korea-America Economic Association, 1987-2002
- International Input-Output Association, 1990-2000

Highlights on Korean Studies:

1. Chinkook Lee, Analysis of U.S.-Korea Agricultural Trade Relations, 1975-2005, A Historical Perspective, *Korea Times*, Washington, DC Edition, October, 2005
2. One of two (John Dyck, the other) from ERS/ USDA among 17 people with expertise on North Korean invited

by the Rockefeller Foundation on September 25, 1997 to discuss how the Foundation could contribute to improved food conditions in North Korea. The group included government officials from the State Department, the U.S. Trade Representative's Office, FAS and ERS/ USDA and university professors.

3. In September, 1990, I was invited by Mr. Selig Harrison, Senior Fellow of the Carnegie Endowment for International Peace, to participate an informal meeting with DPRK Ambassador to United Nations in New York, Mr. Han See Hae. Among the participants there were: Assistant Secretary of State for Far East and Pacific Islanders, Mr. Richard Solomon, CIA North Korea desk officer, John Murray, Intelligence and Research, Department of State, South Korean Embassy Political Attache and others. September, 1990. I also met Mr. Han when I went to Pyongyang for the second time in 1991. He asked me the time in Atlanta at that time. He was interested in inviting former President Jimmy Carter to Pyongyang and wanted to call him.

4. Xinsen Diao, John Dyck, David Skully, Agapi Somwaru, and Chinkook Lee, "South Korea's

5. Agricultural Policy Hampered Economic Growth," *Agricultural Outlook*, ERS/USDA, June-July, 2002, pp. 10-13.

6. Xinshen Diao, John Dyck, Chinkook Lee, and Agapi Somwaru, "Can Reindustrialization of North Korea Support a Sustainable Food Supply?" in *Perspective on Korean Unification and Economic Integration*, p.72-87, Edward Elgar Publishing Inc., May 2001.

7. Chinkook Lee, "An Analysis of North Korea's Economic Development with Special Reference to Agriculture," *Journal of North East Asian Studies*, George Washington University, Fall, 1990, p. 23-33.

8. Chinkook Lee, Agricultural Development and Trade; South Korean Lessons to the Third World, *Asian Review*, Southern Connecticut University, New Haven, Conn., April, 1987.

9. Chinkook Lee and David Culver, "Agricultural Development in Three Asian Countries: A Comparative

Analysis," *Agricultural Economics Research*, U.S. Department of Agriculture, February, 1985.

10. John Dyck, Xinshen Diao, Agapi Somwaru, David Skully, and Chinkook Lee, "Cost of South Korea's Agricultural Policy Choices- A General Equilibrium Analysis," a selected paper presented at the annual meetings of American Agricultural Economics Association, Nashville, Tennessee, August 8-11, 1999.

11. Xinshen Diao, Agapi Somwaru, john Dyck, David Skully, and Chinkook Lee, "South Korea's Agricultural Policy Choices and Their Consequences," a paper presented at the International Agricultural Trade Research Consortium, St. Petersburg Florida, Dec. 14, 1998.

12. Chinkook Lee, "Opportunities and Challenges in Inter-Korean Economic Cooperation: -The Case of Agriculture," a selected paper presented at the 5th Korea-America Economic Association.

13. Chinkook Lee, "An Analysis of North Korea's Attempt at Economic Development: with a special reference to agriculture," a selected presented at the 4th International Korean Economists Conference, Seoul, Korea, August 15-18, 1990.

14. Chinkook Lee, "An Agricultural Development Perspective on Trade Friction: The Case of Three Asian Countries," a selected presented at the 3rd International Conference on Korea Studies, Osaka, Japan, August 2-6, 1990.

15. Chinkook Lee, "The Changing Nature of U.S. - Korean Agricultural Trade: A Development Perspective," a selected paper presented at the Third International Convention of Korea-America Economic Association and Korea Economic Association, Seoul, Korea, August 2-6, 1988.

16. Chinkook Lee and David Culver, "Role of Agriculture in Economic Development in Three Asian Countries," a selected paper presented at the MidAtlantic Association of Asian Studies, University of Pennsylvania, October 2830, 1983.

17. Chinkook Lee, "Comparative Economic Development in Three Asian Countries," a selected paper presented at the

Western Economic Association annual meetings, June 27-July 1, 1980, San Diego, California.

Honors and Awards:

- Economic Research Service, U.S. Department of Agriculture (ERS/USDA); Administrator's Certificate of Merit Award for Publishing the Timely Article, "How Would Increasing the Minimum Wage Affect Food Prices," in the *Current Issues Series*, (Agricultural Information Bulletin #747, June, 2000.
- ERS/USDA; Administrator's Certificate of Merit for "Outstanding Efforts to Promote Workforce Diversity in 1999," May 1999 (and Cash Award).
- ERS/USDA; Certificate of Merit (and Cash Award) for "Conducting solid research on the effects of minimum wage increases on food prices and an excellent timing and publication delivery," June 1999.
- ERS/USDA; Administrator's Certificate of Merit for "Outstanding Efforts to Promote Workforce Diversity in 1998," August 1998.
- Economic Research Service, U.S. Department of Agriculture; Administrator's Certificate of Merit Award for Excellence in Team Research on the Importance of Agricultural Trade for the Rural Economy, Spring, 1997.
- *The Journal of Agricultural Economics Research*, which was founded in 1949, published fourteen of its most significant articles in its final issue (Vol. 45 #4, 1995). These include an article which I co-authored with Gerald Schluter, "Effects of Relative Price Changes on U.S. Food Sectors, 1967-78," which was published by Schluter-Lee in the January 1981 issue.
- Served as one of ten editorial board members of the new ERS publication, *World Agriculture: Current Trends and Perspectives*, 1991.
- ERS/USDA; Administrator's Special Merit Award in Communication for developing a successful "Issues in Agricultural Policy" series that provided a general audience with clear, concise, and timely information relevant to choices in public policy, April, 1988.

- ERS/USDA; Administrator's Creative Economic Analysis and Communication Award, 1981.
- Member of the International Committee, American Agricultural Economics Association, 19831986 nominated by Dr. Neil Harl, President of the AAEA.
- One of two (John Dyck, the other) from ERS/ USDA among 17 people with expertise on North Korean invited by the Rockefeller Foundation on September 25, 1997 to discuss how the Foundation could contribute to improved food conditions in North Korea. The group included government officials from the State Department, the U.S. Trade Representative's Office, FAS and ERS/ USDA and university professors.
- Served as one of ten editorial board members of the new ERS/USDA publication, *World Agriculture: Current Trends and Perspectives*, 1991.
- Numerous cash and spot (bonus) awards.

Other Activities:

- A Member of Self-Development of People Committee, the National Capital Presbytery, 1986-1990.
- President of Korean Economic Society, 1984-1986.
- Member of Board of trustees, The Korean-American Scholarship Foundation in U.S.A, 1983-2001.
- Director of the Korean Education Center of Bethesda, 1983-1984.

Foreign Language Skills:

Fluent in **Korean** with ability to read, write, and translate. Working knowledge of **Chinese** and **Japanese**.

Symposia:

Organizer and presenter of a symposium on "Applications of Input-Output Analysis to Agricultural and Rural Research--Problems and Prospects," American Agricultural Economics Association Meetings, Vancouver, British Columbia, Canada, August 4-8, 1990.

Organizer and moderator of a symposium on "Training Agricultural Economists for the Third World," American Agricultural Economics Association meetings, Cornell University, August 5-8, 1984.

Organizer and a panelist of symposium on "U.S. Agricultural Trade and Agricultural Development in the Third World," American Agricultural Economics Association meetings, Reno, Nevada, July 27-30, 1986.

Book Reviews:

- "Exploring New Frontiers," *The Journal of Agricultural Economic Research*, Fall, 1990, a book review of *Frontiers of Input-Output Analysis*, Edited by Ronald E. Miller, Karen Polenske, and Adam Rose, Oxford University Press, 1989.

- "Trade Theory versus the Real World," *The Journal of Agricultural Economics Research*, Fall 1988, Vol. 40, #4, p.27-28, a book review of *Empirical Methods for International Trade*, edited by Robert C. Feenstra, MIT Press, 1988.

Publications:

1. Gerald Schluter and Chinkook Lee, "The 'New Economy' and efficiency in food market system: A complement or a battleground between economic classes?" *Technology in Society*, 27 (2005) 217-228.
2. Gerald Schluter and Chinkook Lee, "Is There a Link between the Changing Skills of Labor Used in U.S. Processed Food Trade and Rural Employment?" *Journal of Agricultural and Applied Economics*, 36,3 (December 2004):691-703.
3. Gerald Schluter and Chinkook Lee, "Can Rural Employment Benefit From Changing Labor Skills in U.S. Processed Food Trade?," *Rural America*, ERS/USDA Volume 17, Issue 4, Winter, 2002, pp. 38-43.
4. Chinkook Lee, "The Effects of Intermediate Input Price Changes on the Food Prices-An Analysis of From the

Ground Up Effects," *Journal of Agribusiness*, Volume 20, Number 1, Spring 2002, pp. 85-102.

5. Xinsen Diao, John Dyck, David Skully, Agapi Somwaru, and Chinkook Lee, "South Korea's Agricultural Policy Hampered Economic Growth," *Agricultural Outlook*, ERS/USDA, June-July, 2002, pp. 10-13.

6. Chinkook Lee, Gerald Schluter, and Brian O'Roark, "Minimum Wage and food Prices: An Analysis of Price-Pass Through Effects," *International Food and Agribusiness Management Review*, Volume 3, #1, pp. 111-128, July 2001.

7. Xinshen Diao, John Dyck, Chinkook Lee, and Agapi Somwaru, "Can Reindustrialization of North Korea Support a Sustainable Food Supply?" in *Perspective on Korean Unification and Economic Integration*, p.72-87, Edward Elgar Publishing Inc., May 2001.

8. Chinkook Lee and Brian O'Roark, "Minimum Wage and Food Prices," *Current Issues*, Agricultural Information Bulletin #820, ERS/USDA, May 2000.

9. Chinkook Lee and Brian O'Roark, "The Impact of Minimum Wage Increases on Food and Kindred Product Prices," An Analysis of Price Pass-Through," Technical Bulletin, #1877, ERS/USDA, July 1999.

10. Chinkook Lee, Fred Gale, and Gerald Schluter, "Most Jobs Created by Exports is in Medium and High Skill Occupations," *Rural Conditions and Trends:* Volume 9, #3, ERS/USDA, pp. 17-21, June 1999.

11. Chinkook Lee, "Minimum Wage Increases - The Impact on Food Prices," *Agricultural Outlook*, ERS/USDA, April 1999, p. 20.

12. Chinkook Lee and Brian O'Roark, "Minimum Wage Increases Have Little Effect on Prices of Food Away from Home," *Food Review*, ERS/USDA, January/April 1999.

13. Gerald Schluter and Chinkook Lee, "Changing Food Consumption Patterns: Their Effect on the U.S. Food System, 1972-1992," *Food Review*, ERS/USDA, January/April 1999.

14. Chinkook Lee and Gerald Schluter, "The Effect of Trade on the Demand for Skilled and Unskilled Workers," *Economic Systems Research*, Journal of the International

Input-Output Association, Vol. 11, #1, March, 1999, pp 49-65.

15. Gerald Schluter, Chinkook Lee, and Michael LeBlanc, "The Weakening Relationships between Farm and Food Prices," Proceedings, *American Journal of Agricultural Economics*, Vol. 80, #5, Dec., 1998, pp 1134-1138.

16. William Edmondson, Gerald Schluter, and Chinkook Lee, "U.S. Agricultural Trade and Its Impact on the Midwest Rural Economy," in *Global Linkages to the Midwest Economy*, Federal Reserve Bank of Chicago, September 16,1996, pp. 1-9.

17. Chinkook Lee and Gerald Schluter, "Demand-Driven Structural Changes in the U.S. Agribusiness Industry, 1972-1987: An Input-Output Perspective," *Journal of International Food and Agribusiness Marketing*, Vol. 8(1) 1996, pp.1-13.

18. William Edmondson, Lowell Dyson, and Chinkook Lee, "The Food and Fiber System Remains an Important Source of Rural Employment Despite Declining Farm Employment," *Rural Conditions and Trends*, ERS/USDA, July 1996. Vol 7(1), pp.18-21.

19. Chinkook Lee, William Edmondson, and Lowell Dyson, "Agricultural Exports and the Rural Economy in the 1990's," *Rural Conditions and Trends*, op.cit, pp. 22-26.

20. Gerald Schluter and Chinkook Lee, "Changing Food Consumption Patterns, Their Effect on the U.S. Food System, 1972-1987: An Input-Output Perspective," *Journal of Food Distribution Research*, July 1996, pp. 48-55.

21. Chinkook Lee and Michelle Robinson, "Factor Intensity and the Changing Commodity Composition of U.S. Agricultural Trade," U.S. Department of Agriculture, Economic Research Service, *Agricultural Economic Report #683*, May, 1994.

22. Chinkook Lee and Gerald Schluter, "Growth and Structural Changes in the U.S. Food and Fiber System: an Input-Output Perspective," *American Journal of Agricultural Economics*, August, 1993, pp. 666-676.

23. Chinkook Lee, "Growth and Changes in The Structure of The U.S. Agribusiness Industry 1972-1982," *Symposium II Proceedings*, pp. 347-354, International Agribusiness

Management Association, Oxford, England, May 16-19, 1992.

24. Chinkook Lee, "Recent Development in Construction of Input-Output Tables with Use and Make Matrices: an Application to U.S. Agriculture," *Canadian Journal of Agricultural Economics*, Vol. 39, No. 4, December, 1991, pp.795-803.

25. Chinkook Lee and Darryl Wills, "U.S. Has A Comparative Edge," *Agricultural Outlook*, Economic Research Service, USDA, April, 1991, pp. 21-23.

26. Chinkook Lee and Harold Taylor, "Ag Products Expand Fertilizer Trade," *Agricultural Outlook*, Economic Research Service, USDA, August, 1991, pp. 17-18.

27. Chinkook Lee and Gerald Schluter. "Fertilizer Intensity of U.S. Agricultural Exports," *World Agriculture: Current Trends and Perspectives*, Economic Research Service, USDA, July 1991, pp. 26-27.

28. Chinkook Lee, "Growth and Changes in the Structure of the U.S. Agricultural Economy, 1972-1982: an Input-Output Perspective," Economic Systems Research, Journal of International Input-Output Association, Vol. 2, No. 3, 1990, pp. 307-315.

29. Darryl Wills, and Chinkook Lee, "Factor Intensity of U.S. Agricultural Trade," *Agricultural Economic Report #637*, Economic Research Service, USDA, August, 1990.

30. Chinkook Lee, "An Analysis of North Korea's Economic Development With Special Reference to Agriculture," *Journal of North East Asian Studies*, George Washington University, Fall, 1990, p. 23-33.

31. C. Edwin Young, Ben T. Hyberg, J. Michael Price, Wen Huang, Chinkook Lee, Jerry Sharples, and Dan Dvoskin, "Economic Effects of Mandatory Production Controls," *Agricultural Economic Report #595*, Economic Research Service, U.S. Department of Agriculture, March, 1989.

32. Chinkook Lee, Darryl Wills, and Gerald Schluter, "Examining the Leontief Paradox in U.S. Agricultural Trade," *Agricultural Economics*, The Journal of the International Association of Agricultural Economics, Vol. 2, November, 1988, Amsterdam, The Netherlands.

144

33. Chinkook Lee, "The Changing Nature of U.S.-Korean Agricultural Trade: A Development Perspective," *Korea's Economy*, Korea Economic Institute of America, Washington, D.C., Fall, 1988.

34. Chinkook Lee and Darryl Wills, "Effects of Dollar Depreciation on Agricultural Prices and Income," *Agribusiness, an International Journal*, September, 1988.

35. Chinkook Lee, Darryl Wills, and Gerald Schluter, "An Empirical Analysis of The Leontief Paradox in U.S. Agricultural Trade," *Agribusiness, an International Journal*, Vol. 4, #1, January, 1988.

36. Chinkook Lee, Agricultural Development and Trade; South Korean Lessons to the Third World, *Asian Review*, Southern Connecticut University, New Haven, Conn., April, 1987.

37. Chinkook Lee, Gerald Schluter, William Edmondson, and Darryl Wills, "Measuring the Size of the U.S. Food and Fiber System," *Agricultural Economic Report* #566, Economic Research Service, U.S. Department of Agriculture, March, 1987.

38. Gerald Schluter, Chinkook Lee, and William Edmondson, "Income and Employment Generation in the Food and Fiber System," *Agribusiness an International Journal*, Vol. 2, #2, pp.143-158, 1986.

39. Chinkook Lee and David Culver, "Agricultural Development in Three Asian Countries: A Comparative Analysis," *Agricultural Economics Research*, U.S. Department of Agriculture, February, 1985.

40. Gerald Schluter and Gene K. Lee, "Effects of Relative Price Changes on U.S. Food Sectors, 196778," *Agricultural Economics Research*, January, 1981, Vol.33, #1, pp. 112.

41. Gene K. Lee, "Changes in the Structure of the Washington State Economy, 196372:An Input-output Analysis," *Western Journal of Agricultural Economics*, July 1980, pp. 63-71.

42. Gene K. Lee and Gerald Schluter, "The Impacts of Real Multiplier vs Inflationary Effects on Output and Income Generation," *Agricultural Economics Research*, U.S. Department of Agriculture, Vol. 29, #1, 1979.

43. Gerald Schluter and Gene K. Lee, "Is Leontief's Paradox Applicable to U.S. Agricultural Trade?," *Western Journal of*

Agricultural Economics, pp.165-172, Vol. 3 #2, December 1978.

44. Gene K. Lee, Leroy L. Blakeslee, and Walter Butcher, "Effects of Exogenous Price Changes on a Regional Economy: An Input-output Analysis," <u>International Regional Science Review</u>, Vol. 2, #1, pp. 15-27, Nov. 1977.

45. Gene K. Lee, "Energy Intensiveness of Washington Agriculture and the Effects of Increases in Energy Prices on Washington Agriculture," *Agriculture and Energy*, pp.19-23, Academic Press, Inc., 1977, New York, 1977.

46. Norman Whittelesey and Gene K. Lee, "Impacts of Energy Price Changes on Food Costs," *Agricultural Bulletin* #822, College of Agriculture Research Center, Washington State University, April, 1976.

47. Gene K. Lee, Leroy L. Blakeslee, and Walter Butcher, "The Effects of Exogenous Changes in Prices and Final Demand for Wheat and Energy Resources on the Washington Economy," *Technical Bulletin* #85, Agricultural Experiment Station, Washington State University, June, 1976.

48. Norman Whittlesey and Gene K. Lee, "Empirical Analysis of the Impacts of Energy Price Changes on Food Costs", <u>Proceedings</u>, Western Agricultural Economics Assn., 48th Annual Meetings, July, 1975.

49. Chinkook Lee, "Financial Crisis in Local Government in the State of Washington," *Annual Report*, County Commissioners Association, State of Washington, Olympia, Washington, January, 1969.

<u>Selected Reviewed Articles for Journal Editors:</u>

1. December 2001, Chinkook Lee, for the Editor of the *Review of Agricultural Economics*, A journal of American Agricultural Economics Association on "The Contribution of Food Marketing to Expanding Employment, Lower Earnings, and the Cost of Food.."

2. September 23, 1998: Chinkook Lee and Gerald Schluter, for the Editor of *Economic Systems Research, a Journal of*

International Input-Output Association, on productivity, employment growth, and technological change.

3. 1994: Chinkook Lee and Gerald Schluter, for the Editor of AJAE on the import liberalization of agricultural products on an economy, a CGE approach.

4. June 1992: Chinkook Lee, Teresa Sun, and Bob Dobman, for the Editor of AJAE on "Heteroskedasticity and Bias in the Estimated Variances of OLS Coefficients."

5. January, 1992: Chinkook Lee and Gerald Schluter, for the Editor of *Agribusiness, an International Journal*, on employment and income impacts of the food and fiber system.

Contributed Professional Papers Presented:

1. Gerald Schluter and Chinkook Lee, "The 'New Economy' and Efficiency in Food Market System: A complement or a battleground between economic classes?," a selected paper presented at the 25th annual meetings of International Agricultural Economics Association, Durban, South Africa, August 16-22, 2003.

2. Chinkook Lee, "The Impact of Intermediate Input Price Changes on Food Prices- an Analysis of "from the ground up" effects" a selected paper presented at the annual meetings of American Agricultural Economics Association, Long Beach, California, July 28-31, 2002.

3. Chinkook Lee and Gerald Schluter, "Consolidation, Economies of Scale, and the Heckscher-Ohlin Theory of Trade – An Empirical Analysis of U.S. Meat Processing Industry," a selected paper presented at the Symposium of International Trade in Livestock Products, January 18-19, 2002, Auckland New Zealand.

4. Gerald Schluter and Chinkook Lee, "Can Rural Areas Benefit from the Changing Skills of Labor Used in U.S. Food Processing Trade?" a selected paper   presented at the 24th annual meetings of International Agricultural Economics Association, Berlin, Germany, August 13-19, 2000.

5. Chinkook Lee and Gerald Schluter, "An I/O Analysis of Common and Diverse Economic Forces Affecting the

U.S. Processed Food Industry," a selected paper presented at the 13th International Conference on Input-Output Techniques, Macerate, Italy, August 21-25, 2000.

6. Chinkook Lee and Gerald Schluter, "Minimum Wage and Food Prices," Western Economic Association International Meetings, Vancouver, B.C., June 29-July 3, 2000.

7. Gerald Schluter and Chinkook Lee, "The Regional Effect of a Sea Changes in Trade Related Food Processing Skills," Western Regional Science Association Meetings, Hawaii, February 26-March 1, 2000.

8. John Dyck, Xinshen Diao, Agapi Somwaru, David Skully, and Chinkook Lee, "Cost of South Korea's Agricultural Policy Choices- A General Equilibrium Analysis," a selected paper presented at the annual meetings of American Agricultural Economics Association, Nashville, Tennessee, August 8-11, 1999.

9. Gerald Schluter, Chinkook Lee, and Michael LeBlanc, "The Weakening Relationships between Farm and Food Prices," an **invited** paper, Annual Meetings of American Agricultural Economics Association, Salt Lake City, August 2-5, 1998.

10. Chinkook Lee and Gerald Schluter, "Trade, Technology and Labor Productivity Effects on the Demand for Skilled and Unskilled Workers: Implications for Rural Areas," a selected paper, Annual meetings of American Agricultural Economics Association, Salt Lake City, August 2-5, 1998.

11. Chinkook Lee and Darryl S. Wills, "Agricultural Exports and Employment in the Western United States: A Balanced Regional Model," a selected paper presented at the annual meetings of the Western Regional Science Association, Monterey, California, February 18-22, 1998.

12. Xinshen Diao, Agapi Somwaru, john Dyck, David Skully, and Chinkook Lee, "South Korea's Agricultural Policy Choices and Their Consequences," a paper presented at the International Agricultural Trade Research Consortium, St. Petersburg Florida, December 14, 1998.

13. William Edmondson, Gerald Schluter, Chinkook Lee, and Lowell Dyson, "U.S. Agricultural Trade and Its Impact on the Midwest Rural Economy," an **invited** paper presented

at the Global Linkages to the Midwest Economy Workshop, Federal Reserve Bank of Chicago, September 18, 1996.

14. William Edmondson, Chinkook Lee, Gerald Schluter, and Lowell Dyson, "Estimating Agricultural Trade-Related Rural Employment in the 90's," a selected paper presented at the annual meetings of American Agricultural Economics Association, July 28-31, 1996, San Antonio, Texas.

15. Chinkook Lee and Gerald Schluter, "Demand-Driven Structural Changes in The U.S. Agribusiness Industry, 1972-1987: An Input-Output Perspective," a selected paper presented at the annual meetings of American Agricultural Economics Association, Indianapolis, Indiana, August 6-9, 1995.

16. Chinkook Lee, "An Eight-Region Impact Analysis of the Selected Federal Government Programs: A Balanced U.S. Regional Model," a selected paper presented at the annual meetings of Southern Regional Science Association, San Antonio, Texas, April 20-23, 1995.

17. Chinkook Lee, "A Nine-Region Impact Analysis of the Selected Federal Government Programs: A Balanced U.S. Regional Model," a selected paper presented at the 94th European Regional Science Association Meetings, August 22-26, 1994, Groningen, The Netherlands.

18. Chinkook Lee, "Determination of The Input-Output Technological Coefficients Under A system of National Accounts (SNA): Implication for U.S. Agriculture," a selected paper presented at the American Agricultural Economics Association meetings, San Diego, Calif., August 7-10, 1994.

19. Chinkook Lee, Michelle Robinson, and Gerald Schluter, "Factor Intensities and The Changing Pattern of Commodity Composition of U.S. Agricultural Trade," a selected paper presented at the International Conference on the New Dimensions of International Agricultural Trade, June 21-23, 1993, Calabria, Italy.

20. Chinkook Lee, "Opportunities and Challenges in Inter-Korean Economic Cooperation: The Case of Agriculture," a selected paper presented at the 5th Korea-America

Economic Association meetings, Seoul, Korea, August 20-21, 1992.

21. Chinkook Lee, Darryl Wills, Michelle Robinson, and Gerald Schluter, "Factor Intensities and the Changing Pattern of Commodity Composition of U.S. Agricultural Trade," a selected paper presented at the American Agricultural Economics Association meetings, August 10-12, 1992, Baltimore, Maryland.

22. Chinkook Lee, "Growth and Changes in the Structure of the U.S. Agribusiness Industry, 1972-1982: An Input-Output Perspective," a selected paper presented at the International Agribusiness Management Association meetings, Oxford, England, May 16-19, 1992.

23. Chinkook Lee, "An Analysis of North Korea's Attempt at Economic Development: with a special reference to agriculture," a selected presented at the 4th International Korean Economists Conference, Seoul, Korea, August 15-18, 1990.

24. Chinkook Lee, "An Agricultural Development Perspective on Trade Friction: The Case of Three Asian Countries," a selected presented at the 3rd International Conference on Korea Studies, Osaka, Japan, August 2-6, 1990.

25. Chinkook Lee, "Growth and Changes in The Structure of The U.S. Agricultural Economy, 1972 - 1982: An Input-output Perspective," a **plenary** paper presented at the Ninth International Convention of Input-output Techniques, September 4 - 9,1989, Keszthely, Hungary.

26. Chinkook Lee and Agapi Somwaru, "Sources of Structural Changes in U.S. Agriculture, 1972-1982: An Input-output Perspective," a selected paper presented at the American Agricultural Economics Association Meetings, Louisiana State University, Baton Rouge, La., July 31, 1989- August 2, 1989.

27. Ibid, The Joint National Meetings of Operations Research Society of America, Canadian Operational Research Society, and The Institute of Management Sciences, Vancouver, British Columbia, May 8 - 10, 1989.

28. Gerald Schluter, Chinkook Lee, and Darryl Wills, "Factor Intensities and the Commodity Composition of U.S. Agricultural Trade," a selected paper presented at the

American Agricultural Economics Association Meetings, Louisiana State University, Baton Rouge, La., July 31 - August 2, 1989.

29. Chinkook Lee, Darryl Wills, and Agapi Somwaru, "Sources of Structural Changes in U.S. Agriculture, 1972-1982: Implications for Agriculture in Western United States," a selected paper presented at the Western Agricultural Economics Association Meetings, Coeur d'Alene, Idaho, July 12, 1989.

30. Gerald Schluter, William Edmondson, and Chinkook Lee, "Rural Communities' Stake in Agricultural Trade," a selected paper presented at the Southern Regional Science Association meetings, April 14-16, 1988, Morgantown, West Virginia.

31. Chinkook Lee, "The Changing Nature of U.S. - Korean Agricultural Trade: A Development Perspective," a selected paper presented at the Third International Convention of Korea-America Economic Association and Korea Economic Association, Seoul, Korea, August 2-6, 1988.

32. Chinkook Lee and Darryl Wills, "Effects of Dollar Depreciation on Agricultural Prices and Income," a selected paper presented at the International Agricultural Economics Association Meetings, Buenos Aires, Argentina, August 24-31, 1988.

33. Ibid, Western Agricultural Economics Association Meetings, Honolulu, Hawaii, July 8-13, 1988.

34. Chinkook Lee and Darryl Wills, "Examining Leontief Paradox in the U.S. Food and Fiber System," a selected paper presented at the American Agricultural Economics Assn. Meetings, August 13, 1987, Michigan State University, E. Lansing, Michigan.

35. Chinkook Lee and David Culver, "Role of Agriculture in Economic Development in Three Asian Countries," a selected paper presented at the MidAtlantic Association of Asian Studies, University of Pennsylvania, October 28-30, 1983.

36. Chinkook Lee, "Price and Income Effect of Devaluation, A Case Study of South Korea," a selected paper presented

at the American Agricultural Economics Association annual meetings, Champaign, Illinois, July 28-31, 1980.

37. Chinkook Lee, "Comparative Economic Development in Three Asian Countries," a selected paper presented at the Western Economic Association annual meetings, June 27-July 1, 1980, San Diego, California.

38. Gene K. Lee, "Changes in Interindustry Demand in Washington State Economy; 1963-1972," a selected paper presented at the Western Economic Association annual meetings, June 1721, 1979.

39. Gene K. Lee, "Seasonal Variations in Prices Paid by Farmers," a selected paper presented at the Southern Agricultural Economics Association, annual meetings, Hot Springs, Arkansas, April 25, 1978.

40. Gene K. Lee and Gerald Schluter, "The Differential Effects of Inflation on Selected Food-Related Sectors of the U.S. Economy, 1967-1976," a selected paper presented at the Western Economic Association meetings, Anaheim, Calif., July 3-6, 1978.

41. Gene K. Lee and Gerald Schluter, "Forecasting Gross Farm Product Through a Macroeconometric Model," a selected paper presented at the Western Economic Association annual meetings, June 1923, 1977, Anaheim, California.

42. Gerald Schluter and Gene K. Lee, "Factor Intensity of American Agricultural Trade," a selected paper presented at the American Agricultural Economics Association annual meetings, July 31-August 3, 1977, San Diego, California.

43. Gerald Schluter and Gene K. Lee, "The Differential Effects of Inflation on Selected Food Related Sectors of the U.S. Economy, 1967-1976," a selected paper presented at the Western Economic Association annual meetings, June 24-27, 1976, San Francisco, California.

44. Gene K. Lee, Leroy L. Blakeslee, and Walter Butcher, "The Effects of Exogenous Changes in Prices and Final Demand for Wheat and Energy Resources on the Washington Economy: An Input-Output Analysis," a selected paper presented at the Western Economic

Association annual meetings, June 24-27, 1976, San Francisco, California.

45. Gene K. Lee and Gerald Schluter, "Real Multiplier vs Inflationary Effects in an Input-Output Model," a selected paper presented at the American Agricultural Economics Association annual meetings, August 15-18, 1976, State College, Pennsylvania.

46. Gene K. Lee and Norman K. Whittlesey, "Potential Impacts of Energy Price Changes on Consumer Food Costs," a selected paper presented at the American Agricultural Economics.

47. Gene K. Lee, Leroy L. Blakeslee, and Walter Butcher, "A Consideration of Exogenous Changes in Prices in a Regional Input-Output Model," a selected paper presented at the Southern Regional Science Association annual meetings, April 25-27, 1975, Atlanta, Georgia.

Selected Staff Analyses:

SA 98-030, November, 1997: Chinkook Lee, Gerald Schluter, and Darryl Wills, comments on "Trade and The American Workers (chapter 6)," of the Economic Report of the President to Keith Collins, Chief Economist, USDA. We found some errors in the report and our comments were incorporated in the final report.

July, 1996: Chinkook Lee, on "Output and Employment and Multipliers," for the Rural Development Administration and Rural Utilities Services, USDA. I provided them output and employment multipliers for selected industries which they used for budgeting for their new construction and utility loans.

SA96-108, December, 1995: Chinkook Lee, on "The Role and Contribution of Agribusiness to U.S. Economy," through Keith Collins, Chief Economist to Secretary's office for Secretary's speech at the Harvard Business School.

October 1993: Ken Hanson and Chinkook Lee, on intersectional analysis of international trade at the request of Sherman Robinson who was a CEA staff. Our report was based on a recent AJAE article by Chinkook Lee and Gerald Schluter on structural changes in the U.S. food and fiber industries. Our reports to Sherman Robinson were quoted in the United States in the World Economy (Chapter 6) of the *Economic Report of the President, 1994.*

SA 92-210, February 10, 1992: Chinkook Lee, on "The importance of the Cattle (Beef) industry to U.S. Agriculture and the U.S. Economy," CED (Commodity Economics Division) prepared the document to Dan Sunmer, Assistant Secretary for Economics through Keith Collins, Chief Economist. I prepared for ARED (Agricultural and Rural Economy Division) package to cover employment and income effects of cattle industry to U.S. economy.

1993: To ERS Administrator, Chinkook Lee, "The Importance of the Broiler Industry and Eating and Drinking Demand in the U.S. Economy."

1989: To ERS Administrator, "Exporting Processed Instead of Raw Agricultural Products."

ACKNOWLEDGMENTS

As I have written about in this memoir, many people influenced my life tremendously in the turning points of my life, and I would like to additionally acknowledge them here.

Dr. Chang Keun Chung in An-Dong, Kyung-Sang Book-Do, Korea helped my Christian faith to grow when both he and I were at Keisung High School in Taegu.

Former president of Soongsil University, Dr. & Rev. Shungnak Luke Kim, went with me to the U.S. Embassy in Seoul, Korea to swear in as my financial sponsor in the U.S. when I was proceeding with study-abroad documents. He also gave me a small note to take to Rev. Noh in Los Angeles. who helped me as I started my life in America. Both are deceased now, but I owe them tremendously for their help at the initial stage of my new life in America.

Vanderbilt University helped me significantly in the beginning of my student life. The university offered me some financial help and part-time employment, and most importantly issued me an I-20 form at the beginning of my study abroad. Without the I-20 form from Vanderbilt, I couldn't have processed my study abroad at the U.S. embassy in Seoul.

Elder and Mrs. Chang Ho Hong, my hometown friend in North Korea, arranged me for a blind date in Los Angeles with my wife and that arrangement was a success. I'm very thankful for their suggesting this arrangement.

In terms of my terminal degree at Washington State University, two professors' commitments in advising and assisting me academically was crucial. Professor Lee Blakeslee, one of the most brilliant economists in the country, was my original dissertation advisor and after accepting my request, sat down with me one day in a faculty room discussing the modeling of my dissertation. Without his initial suggestions and help, I would not have been able to start writing the dissertation. Professor Walt Butcher accepted my request to be my next dissertation advisor and helped me to get through finishing my degree. He also helped me find employment at Economic Research Service, USDA where I spent my entire career.

My colleague Gerald Schluter in ERS/USDA, with whom I spent my entire career in USDA, was very helpful polishing my English when I was finalizing my papers to publish and our countless discussions on economic Issues throughout our careers were very memorable. I thank him for his friendship and professional assistance.

Samuel Rose was a Washington, D.C. real estate investor who met my wife at Bender Building while she was operating the lobby shop, then offered a cafe space in a new building he had built, ready to operate with all equipment set up. So we were able to make money as soon as the cafe was open. He also gave my wife another bigger cafe space in the next new building he built adjacent to the previous. This building had the CNN Washington bureau as a tenant, so we had heavy traffic in and out and were profitable as soon as we opened. One summer, we were even able go to his summer house in Key West for vacation without paying any rent. Many thanks to Mr. Rose for his support.

Finally, two additional people who influenced major turning points of my life are Father Paul D. Lee in Maryland and his elder brother Matthew Lee who became my Christian Father. As I expressed in the memoir, I had difficulties with my Christian life as an adult, and my conversion to Catholicism settled me down in my faith. With these two spiritual leaders' help, I'm happy to say that my spiritual life has stabilized and been strengthened. All glory to God!

ABOUT THE AUTHOR

Chinkook Lee is a first-generation Korean immigrant who originally was a refugee from North Korea. He was educated in both South Korea and the United States and spent nearly 30 years in civil service as an economic researcher with the U.S. Department of Agriculture. He lives in Aliso Viejo, California with his beloved wife of more than 50 years, Kum. He has two grown children and five grandchildren.

74294266R00097

Made in the USA
San Bernardino, CA
14 April 2018